Kulturen im Dialog V - Culture in Dialogo V - Cultures in Dialogue V

INTERKULTURELLER DIALOG

Herausgegeben von Annemarie Profanter

BAND 8

PETER LANG

Annemarie Profanter (Hrsg.)

Kulturen im Dialog V
Culture in Dialogo V
Cultures in Dialogue V

Fünftes JungakademikerInnen-Forum in Südtirol
Quinto Forum per Neolaureati in Alto Adige
Fifth Forum for Young Graduates in South Tyrol

PETER LANG

Bibliografische Information der Deutschen Nationalbibliothek
Die Deutsche Nationalbibliothek verzeichnet diese Publikation
in der Deutschen Nationalbibliografie; detaillierte bibliografische
Daten sind im Internet über http://dnb.d-nb.de abrufbar.

Umschlagabbildung:
© Rienzner Martina / Xishuangbanna in Yunnan (China), 2010

ISSN 1866-752X
ISBN 978-3-631-77806-7 (Print)
E-ISBN 978-3-631-78194-4 (E-PDF)
978-3-631-78195-1 (EPUB)
978-3-631-78196-8 (MOBI))
DOI 10.3726/b15290

© Peter Lang GmbH
Internationaler Verlag der Wissenschaften
Berlin 2019
Alle Rechte vorbehalten.

Peter Lang – Berlin · Bern · Bruxelles ·
New York · Oxford · Warszawa · Wien

Diese Publikation wurde begutachtet.

www.peterlang.com

Annemarie Profanter

Vorwort

"They will only see Italy in a postcard" with these words Matteo Salvini, the far-right interior minister and Lega leader of Italy, in 2018 describes his agenda of "stopping immigration" (Stickings, 2018). Harbours were shut to NGO ships and a policy of non-dialogue was initiated in June of 2018. Alarming scenes of over-loaded vessels and announcements of inhumane measures are at the forefront of Italy's political agenda. The permeability of the country's physical borders has made international migration a challenging reality. Concerns focus on the pos-sibility of a large uncontrolled wave of migration accompanied by chaotic scenes in the immigrant holding centres on the Italian islands of Lampedusa and Sicily which are pictured as being overwhelmed with African immigrants. The public discourse centres around waves of migration assaulting 'Fortress Europe'.

What has happened as a consequence of all these developments? Much is changing on the local, regional and EU-level, impacting the on-going processes of transnational migration and mobility.

This political turmoil has challenged dominant and essentialist modes of thin-king about immigration while at the same time affecting European government policy on immigration. Previous policies had encouraged authoritarian regimes such as Libya to constrain immigration. Now, attention is turning to ways that Southern Europe can shield its borders and assist in the maintenance of social stability without recourse to the previously accepted authoritarian notions of sta-bility. The polarizing strategies present in either the authoritarian republics or rentier monarchies.

Discoursive strategies are adopted to construct shared collective identities based on an atmosphere of fear and defense. All of a sudden it seems socially acceptable to "shut the door" in the face of people suffering in multiple ways. A public discourse of exclusion seems to be pervasive. To overstate the case: the drowning of people in the Mediterranean is viewed as warranted to maintain the status quo by a certain strata of society. The ideologies of radical right populism will continue to show effects on immigration policy in Italy and Europe.

European governments need to rethink policies of immigration that fos-ter integration of minorities and take religious traditions into account. "Both the difficulties of [...] immigrant groups in adapting to European norms and institutions and the xenophobic and authoritarian reactions within the state institutions and majority societies challenge the quality and stability of European democracies" (Somer and Tol, 2010, p. 4). Most states today have a multicultural demographic, and intercultural dialogue is key in addressing ethnic diversity within the state.

Der Dialog der Kulturen steht auch im Mittelpunkt der Betrachtungen dieses Sammelbandes. Es findet ein interkultureller Austausch auf mehreren Ebenen statt: persönlich, thematisch und in Bezug auf verschiedene disziplinäre Ansätze. Der Sammelband ist in vier thematische Cluster gegliedert: 1) Transnational ties and movement; 2) Identität; 3) Diritti sospesi tra bisogno e desiderio; 4) Dialogue of languages and dialogue through the language.

Im *ersten thematischen Cluster* beschäftigen sich die beiden Autor*innen Daniela Gruber und Dennis Fricken mit *transnationalen Räumen*: Sie beschreiben Orte und Netzwerke, die über nationalstaatliche Grenzen hinausreichen, und in denen Interaktionen stattfinden, die diese Grenzen überwinden und überschreiten.

Im Falle von **Dennis Fricken** ist dies ein Dorf im Hohen Atlasgebirge in Marokko, *Oukaïmeden*. Es handelt sich dabei um eine von Berbern gegründete Siedlung, die in einer bis dato überwiegend landwirtschaftlich geprägten Region liegt, und in welcher in den letzten Jahren sowohl von Marokkaner*innen als auch von Menschen aus anderen Ländern, wie beispielsweise Frankreich, eine hohe Anzahl an Zweitwohnsitzen begründet wurde. Fricken beschäftigt sich in seinem Beitrag anhand einer vor Ort durchgeführten Fallstudie mit der Frage, wie dieses in der Fachliteratur als „Amenity Migration" bezeichnete Phänomen, die Gemeinde verändert. Die Fragestellung lautet: Welche sozio-ökonomischen, demographischen, kulturellen und Settlement-Veränderungen zeigen sich angesichts der Newcomer?

Ausgehend von einer Fallstudie wurden Expert*inneninterviews durchgeführt, problemfokussierte und standardisierte Interviews, ein standardisierter Fragebogen sowie *geographic mapping* eingesetzt. Das Sample setzt sich aus 19 Probanden zusammen, sogenannte „Einheimische" bzw. „Berber". Die Daten wurden anhand der Qualitativen Inhaltsanalyse nach Mayring ausgewertet.

Die Ergebnisse zeigen, dass die Präsenz der Zweitwohnbesitzer*innen in erster Linie zu einer räumlichen Teilung des Dorfes geführt hat: Auf der einen Seite ist eine, mit besserer Infrastruktur, ausgestattete Siedlung entstanden, in der die neu zugezogenen, saisonalen Migrant*innen wohnen; auf der anderen Seite gibt es nach wie vor die Siedlung der Berber*innen, die nicht über die Infrastruktur der Zweitwohnbesitzer*innen verfügt. Diese soziale Trennung setzt sich auch auf der Ebene der Interaktionen fort: Diese sind überwiegend darauf beschränkt, dass viele Zweitwohnbesitzer*innen sogenannte *gardeurs* angestellt haben, welche sich um ihr Haus kümmern. Ansonsten gibt es, wie Fricken festhält, kaum einen Austausch. Insgesamt ist so durch die Präsenz der Zweitwohnbesitzer*innen zwar ein Ort mit transnationalen Verbindungen entstanden, die Lebensweisen und -bedingungen der bisher dort ansässigen Berber*innen haben sich aber – bis auf ein paar kleinere zusätzliche Einkommensquellen – kaum verändert.

Der Autor kommt zum Schluss, dass auch sonst keine die Lebensbedingungen verbessernde Infrastruktur entstanden ist, also keine Krankenhäuser, Schulen oder Ähnliches. Gleichzeitig sind aber die Grundstückspreise gestiegen, was – laut den Schlussfolgerungen des Autors – für die Berber nicht weiter ein Problem darstellt, allerdings die Frage aufwirft, warum dies so ist: Wie sieht es mit dem Grundstückserwerb der Berber aus?

Intensiveren Austausch und ein weit aus höheres Maß an Interaktion gibt es zwischen den Akteuren in **Daniela Gruber**s Beitrag. Auf folgende theoretische Konzepte wird dabei Bezug genommen: *transnationalism from below, ethnoscapes Appadurai.*

Sie beschäftigt sich aus einer kultur- und sozialanthropligischen Perspektive mit transnationalen religiösen Netzwerken von Roma und Sinti, die in Interaktion mit der Katholischen Kirche treten – eine Organisation, die ebenso transnationalen Verbindungen aufweist. Beide treffen jährlich in zwei großen Wallfahrten in Saintes Maries de la Mer in Frankreich und Mariazell in Österreich aufeinander, mit denen sich Gruber in Form von zwei Fallstudien auseinandergesetzt hat.

Es wurden qualitative Interviews und teilnehmende Beobachtung eingesetzt. Die Datenauswertung erfolgte in Anleitung an Flicks Methode des thematischen Kodierens.

Im Ergebnis zeigt ihre Arbeit einen ungleichen Dialog zwischen der Katholischen Kirche und Netzwerken von Roma und Sinti. Während sie auf lokaler Ebene, bei den Wallfahrten, einen konstruktiven und von Vertrauen geprägten Austausch zwischen Vertreter*innen der katholischen Kirche und Roma sowie Sinti beobachten konnte, sind offizielle Dokumente der Katholischen Kirche nach wie vor von Stereotypen und einem „Othering" gegenüber Roma und Sinti geprägt. So wird beispielsweise in offiziellen Dokumenten die angebliche nomadische Lebensweise verurteilt.

Beide Beiträge zeigen: Globale Ungleichheiten wirken in transnationalen Räumen und Netzwerken fort. Im Falle von Frickens Studie, profitiert v.a. eine Seite (die Zweitwohnbesitzer*innen) von der zunehmenden Transnationalität des Ortes *Oukaïmeden;* im Falle von Grubers Studie ändert auch ein auf lokaler Ebene stattfindender produktiver Austausch zwischen Katholischer Kirche,

Roma und Sinti, nichts daran, dass trotzdem nach wie vor in offiziellen Dokumenten der Katholischen Kirche Roma und Sinti herabsetzende Stereotypen
reproduziert werden.

An diese Auseinandersetzung mit transnationalen Räumen schließen im
darauffolgenden *zweiten thematischen Cluster* die Beiträge von Roberta Rosa
und Federica Pastore an. Beide beschäftigen sich mit der Frage, wie *Identitäten*
im grenzüberschreitenden, also transnationalen Raum der Europäischen Union
verhandelt werden. Im ersten Fall, im politikwissenschaftlichen Beitrag von
Roberta Rosa, stehen drei Regionen im Mittelpunkt, in denen es mithilfe von
EU-Kooperationsvereinbarungen gelungen ist eine länderübergreifende Zusammenarbeit von nationalen Minderheiten zu etablieren. Es handelt sich dabei um
die *Europaregion Tirol-Südtirol-Trentino*, die *EGTC Pons Danubii* (Ungarn und
Slowakei) und die *Region Sønderjylland-Schleswig* (Dänemark – Deutschland) –
alle drei historisch umkämpfte Regionen, in denen nationale Minderheiten
leben, die durch Grenzen voneinander getrennt wurden. Rosas Analyse der drei
Grenzen überschreitenden Kooperationsvereinbarungen und deren Umsetzung
in die Praxis zeigt, dass es – trotz aller Unterschiedlichkeit in der Ausgestaltung –
gelungen ist in allen drei Regionen ein Mehr an Zusammenarbeit und Austausch
zu fördern sowie Grenzen überschreitende, in der Region (nicht in der Nation)
verortete, Identitätsangeboten zu stärken.

Federica Pastore richtet in ihrem sprachwissenschaftlichen Beitrag den Blick
auf eine andere Gruppe von Minderheiten in der Europäischen Union, auf sogenannte „Neue Minderheiten", Migrant*innen aus Drittstaaten, die nach Europa
zugezogen sind. Während seitens der Europäischen Union den „alten", regional
verorteten, Minderheiten, die im Zentrum Rosas Beitrag stehen, gewisse Rechte
zuerkannt werden, ist dies bei den „Neuen Minderheiten" kaum der Fall. Im
Vordergrund steht hier die Forderung nach Integration, eine Forderung die
häufig einseitig formuliert wird: Integrieren sollen sich die Neuzugezogenen,
die Mehrheitsgesellschaft hingegen leistet dabei kaum einen Beitrag. So ist es
auch im Falle von Sprachenrechten, mit welchen sich Pastore in ihrem Beitrag
im Detail beschäftigt. Die *Europäische Charta der Regional- und Minderheitensprachen* sieht Rechte für Sprecher*innen regionaler Minderheitensprachen
vor, so beispielsweise die Möglichkeit Regional- oder Minderheitensprachen
bei regionalen Behörden verwenden zu können oder das Recht auf Unterricht
in der Erstsprache. Dies gilt aber nicht für die Sprachen neu in die Europäische Union zugezogener Menschen; im Gegenteil, im öffentlichen Diskurs wird
immer wieder die These vertreten, eine Förderung der Erstsprache behindere
den Erwerb der Mehrsprache. Auf Basis einer Auseinandersetzung mit
Forschungsliteratur zu diesem Thema gelingt es Pastore in ihrem Beitrag diese

Annahme/These zu widerlegen, und aufzuzeigen, dass eine über reine Symbolik hinausreichende Anerkennung der „Neuen Minderheitensprachen" seitens der Europäischen Union, aber auch seitens ihrer Mitgliedsstaaten, integrationsfördernd wirken könnte. Dies nicht nur deshalb, weil Erstsprachenförderung den Erwerb der Mehrheitssprache erleichtert, sondern auch, weil Sprache mehr als reines Kommunikationsmittel ist. Wie Pastore aufzeigt, werden über Sprache auch Identitäten verhandelt sowie gesellschaftliche Ein- und Ausschlüsse durch das Garantieren bzw. Nicht-Garantieren von Sprachenrechten praktiziert. Eine Anerkennung der in die Europäische Union mitgebrachten sprachlichen Ressourcen würde so für neu zugezogenen Menschen einerseits ein Mehr an gesellschaftliche Teilhabe, andererseits aber auch eine Anerkennung ihrer selbst bedeuten – beides unabdingbare Grundlagen für einen Austausch auf Augenhöhe und somit auch Voraussetzung dafür, dass Integration gelingen kann.

Mit Rechten, deren Zuerkennung bzw. Nicht-Zuerkennung, beschäftigen sich auch die Autor*innen im ***dritten thematischen Cluster „Diritti sospesi tra bisogno e desiderio"***. Alle drei Beiträge setzen sich mit Lebenssituationen auseinander, in denen grundlegende menschliche Bedürfnisse aufgrund von rechtlichen Barrieren zeitweise oder auch permanent unerfüllt bleiben. Bei **Enrico Battaglia** sind dies die Bedürfnisse von Asylsuchenden in Italien, insbesondere der Wunsch in der neuen Umgebung ankommen zu können, Arbeit zu haben und an der Gesellschaft teilhaben zu können, welcher – solange über das laufende Asylverfahren nicht entschieden wurde – im Wartemodus auf Erfüllung wartet. In seinem Beitrag beschreibt Battaglia, wie er sich als Grafikdesigner dieser Lebenssituation in Form von Teilnehmender Beobachtung in einer Unterbringung für Asylsuchende angenähert hat und wie er später die vorgefundenen Lebensbedingungen, v.a. den Status des Wartens, die gesellschaftlichen Isolation bis auf durch die Unterkunft organisierte Begegnungen beispielsweise in Form von Sprachkursen und die Regulierung bzw. Überwachung des Alltagslebens in Form einer *Grafik Novel* mit dem Titel „Fuori di qui" einem breiteren Publikum zugänglich gemacht hat. Diese *Grafik Novel* ist in drei Teile gegliedert: 1) Erzählung/narrazione principale (blu); 2) Tagebuch/diario personale (rosso); 3) Vignetten von Gesetzestexten. Die graphischen Elemente sollen den Zustand des Wartens abbilden, so stehen z.B. leere Seiten sinnbildlich für Leere, Langeweile, Warten.

Marcella Cometti zeigt im darauffolgenden Beitrag, dass diese Situation des Wartens auf Erfüllung grundlegender Bedürfnisse, auch nach positivem Ausgang des Asylverfahrens fortdauern kann. So beispielsweise, das Recht auf Familie, mit welchem sie sich in ihrem rechtswissenschaftlichen Beitrag beschäftigt. Das Fremdenrecht sieht in Italien, wie auch in anderen europäischen Ländern, zwar Familienzusammenführungen vor; Menschen, die dieses in Anspruch neh-men wollen, werden aber mit mehreren Hürden konfrontiert. Dazu gehört, dass die rechtliche Definition dessen, was als eine Familie gilt – wer dazugehört, und wer nicht – häufig nicht den Lebenssituationen von geflüchteten Familien ent-spricht. So gelten beispielsweise Kinder von verstorbenen oder verschwundenen Verwandten, die angenommen wurden, nicht als Teil der Kernfamilie. Für sie kann kein Recht auf Familienzusammenführung in Anspruch genommen wer-den. Hinzu kommen lange Wartezeiten auf Entscheidungen nach Anträgen. Wie Cometti festhält, betragen diese je nach Land zwischen 18 und 24 Monate. Dies sind Monate in denen viele Schutzberechtigte in großer Sorge um ihre Ange-hörigen leben, die sich nach wie vor in einer gefährlichen Umgebung befinden.

Cometti und Battaglia beschreiben beide Situationen in denen Menschen grundlegende Rechte, wie das Recht auf Arbeit oder das Recht auf Familie, ver-wehrt werden, weil deren Inanspruchnahme in einem Spannungsverhältnis mit nationalstaatlichen Interessen (Grenzschutz, Angst vor hohen Einwanderungs-zahlen) stehen. Grund- und Menschenrechte, die eigentlich unbegrenzt gültig sein sollten, werden so begrenzt und/oder zeitweise aufgehoben. Deren Inan-spruchnahme wird auf ein (oft unbekanntes) Später verschoben, und an eng definierte Kriterien gebunden.

Etwas anders gelagert ist die Situation, die **Stefano Piccioni** in seinem Beitrag beschreibt. Er beschäftigt sich mit dem Recht auf Sexualität von Menschen mit Behinderung in Italien, welches ebenso oft nicht in Anspruch genommen werden kann, und in den Bereich eines unerfüllten Wunsches rückt. Die Gründe dafür liegen aber nicht in nationalstaatlichen Interessen, sondern überwiegend an einer gesellschaftlichen Tabuisierung, welche verhindert, dass rechtliche Rahmenbedin-gungen für eine Professionalisierung von „assistenza sessuale" (Sexualassistenz) geschaffen werden. Sexuelle Assistenz bezeichnet professionell angeleitete Metho-den wie beispielsweise Massagen, Streicheln, Spiele um den eigenen Körper zu ent-decken. Während es in anderen europäischen Ländern, wie in den Niederlanden, in Deutschland oder in Österreich, in den letzten Jahren gelungen ist Ausbildungs-lehrgänge, Ethik- und Berufskodizes sowie Supervisionsangebote für Menschen zu schaffen, die professionelle Sexualassistenz bzw. -begleitung für Menschen mit Behinderung anbieten, ist dies in Italien nicht der Fall. 2016 wurde zwar ein ent-sprechender Gesetzesentwurf vorgelegt, welcher ein Ausbildungscurriculum und eine Definition des Berufsbildes beinhaltete, bis zur Fertigstellung von Piccionis Beitrags im Jänner 2018 wurde über diesen aber noch nicht entschieden. Wie Pic-cioni auf der Grundlage von Interviews mit Pflegekräften aufzeigt, wird sexuelle Assistenz in der Zwischenzeit in einen Graubereich ohne ethische und gesetzliche Richtlinien, die Orientierung bieten und schützen würden, verlagert.

Den Abschluss bildet das *vierte Cluster „Dialogue of languages and dialogue through the language"* mit zwei sprachwissenschaftlichen Beiträgen von Mihaela Mihova und Valerio Fidenzi. Hier geht es nicht mehr um die Rechte bzw. Rechtsansprüche gesellschaftlich marginalisierter Gruppen, sondern um Begegnungen mit dem sogenannten Anderen und daraus entstehenden Vorstellungen. Diese Begegnungen finden in beiden Fällen vermittelt über Sprache statt. Bei **Mihaela Mihova** ist dies der Spracherwerb und damit verbundene Vorstellungen über die neu erlernte Sprache und deren Sprecher*innen, mit denen sie sich im Detail anhand des Beispiels von schwedischen Schüler*innen, die sich in ihrer Schullaufbahn für Deutsch als Fremdsprache entschieden haben, beschäftigt. Ihre auf Basis von qualitativen Interviews gewonnenen Ergebnisse zeigen zwei unterschiedliche Perspektiven der Schüler*innen auf das Deutsche: Einerseits ist für die Schüler*innen Deutsch v.a. aufgrund eines angenommenen instrumentellen Nutzens als Fremdsprache attraktiv. Deutsch – so die Aussagen der Schüler*innen – könne künftig bei Reisen, aber auch bei der Jobsuche nützlich sein. Andererseits reproduzierten die Schüler*innen in den geführten Interviews weit verbreite Stereotypen über das Deutsch und über den amtlich deutschsprachigen Raum: Deutsch klinge „hart", „aggressiv" und „grob" und wird überwiegend mit Deutschland, deutschen Automarken, Speisen wie Wurst oder Schnitzel, sowie weiters auch mit Nazis und dem Zweiten Weltkrieg in Verbindung gebracht. Gleichzeitig aber reflektierten die Schüler*innen diese Äußerungen in weiterer Folge und bezeichneten diese selbst als stereotype Vorstellungen, die sich aus dem Konsum unterschiedlicher Medien speisen, die ebenso auch widerlegt werden können.

Mit einem solchen, wenn auch weniger reflektierten Sprechen über Andere beschäftigt sich auch **Valerio Fidenzi** in seinem Beitrag. Er analysiert einen umfangreichen Korpus bestehend aus 163 Zeitungsartikeln, die von 1816 bis 1949 in britischen Zeitungen über die im Südatlantik gelegene Insel *Tristan da Cunha* (damals britische Kolonie) veröffentlicht wurden. Die Ergebnisse seiner Diskursanalyse zeigen, dass *Tristan da Cunha* im 19. Jahrhundert kaum Aufmerksamkeit seitens der britischen Medien erfahren hat; dies spiegelt die geographische, aber auch sozio-ökonomische Isolation wieder, in der sich die Insel damals befand. Diese überwiegende Unsichtbarkeit veränderte sich jedoch zu Beginn des 20. Jahrhunderts, und wich einem – die Bevölkerung *Tristan da Cunhas* und deren Lebensbedingungen idealisierenden – Bild, welches die tatsächlichen sehr prekären Lebensumstände ausblendete. Diese Imagination eines fernen, abgelegenen Ortes blieb in den Zeitschriften bis zu Beginn des Ersten Weltkrieges präsent; dann verschwand Tristan da Cunha angesichts anderer weltpolitischer Themen wieder in einer medialen Unsichtbarkeit.

La piattaforma „Culture in dialogo", nata dalla necessità di dare a neolaureati e neodottori di ricerca uno spazio di scambio interdisciplinare e discussione, è giunta alla sua quinta edizione. A cominciare dall'anno accademico 2006–2007 il numero dei neolaureati e neodottori di ricerca che hanno fatto parte di questa iniziativa è cresciuto anno dopo anno e assieme ad esso si può anche osservare un certo sviluppo tematico e del discorso interculturale. Per questo ciclo si sono candidati neolaureati e neodottori di ricerca di diverse discipline, con un totale di 60 tesi di „neo-esperti" che affrontavano il tema da diversi punti vista scientifici. Le cinque migliori tesi selezionate dalla commissione multidisciplinare sono state presentate al pubblico nel novembre 2017 (vd. foto). La commissione ha poi scelto tra queste l'opera più innovativa ed interessante e premiato pertanto la dissertazione dottorale di Julia Sonnleitner sul tema "Apartheid was a faraway country. What memory studies can learn about interpretive frameworks of race and culture from the South African context". Questo lavoro sarà pubblicato come monografia per la casa editrice Peter Lang, mentre gli altri lavori particolarmente interessanti e innovativi vengono pubblicati per sunto in questa raccolta di articoli.

© 2017 Annemarie Profanter
Premiazione della vincitrice del Quinto Forum per Neolaureati 2017 alla Facoltà di Scienze della Formazione della Libera Università di Bolzano
Da sinistra a destra: Martina Rienzner, Stefan Glüher, Walter Schicho, Annemarie Profanter, Julia Sonnleitner, Daniela Gruber, Veronica Spano, Marcella Cometti, Anna Aluffi-Pentini, Walter Lorenz.

Premiazione della vincitrice del Quinto Forum per Neolaureati 2017 alla Facoltà di Scienze della Formazione della Libera Università di Bolzano
Da sinistra a destra: Martina Rienzner, Stefan Glüher, Walter Schicho, Annemarie Profanter, Julia Sonnleitner, Daniela Gruber, Veronica Spano, Marcella Cometti, Anna Aluffi-Pentini, Walter Lorenz.

Come tutta l'initiativa anche questa curatela è trilingue: il lettore troverà testi in italiano, tedesco e inglese. Il comitato scientifico rispecchia questa pluralità non solo linguistica ma anche di tradizioni accademiche ed è composto dai seguenti professori delle Università di Bolzano, Vienna, Roma Tre:

- Prof. Walter Lorenz, Rettore della Libera Università di Bolzano
- Prof. Gerhard Glüher, Facoltà di Design e Arti, della Libera Università di Bolzano
- Prof. Walter Schicho, Istituto di Sviluppo Internazionale, Università di Vienna
- Prof.ssa Anna Aluffi-Pentini, Facoltà di Scienze della Formazione, Libera Università di Bolzano e Università degli Studi Roma Tre
- Prof. Stefan Franz Schubert, Facoltà di Economia, Libera Università di Bolzano
- Mag. Martina Rienzner, Studi Africani, Università di Vienna
- Prof.ssa Annemarie Profanter, Facoltà di Scienze della Formazione, Libera Università di Bolzano

Colgo l'occasione per ringraziare di cuore coloro che insieme a me hanno sostenuto con il loro contributo intellettuale questa iniziativa e vissuto nelle numerose riunioni il dialogo tra le culture accademiche e culturali. Senza la loro disponibilità ad accogliere e interpretare ogni lavoro scientifico con una lente disciplinare particolare, l'esito del nostro lavoro non sarebbe stato così pluralistico, vario e stimolante.

I veri protagonisti di questa iniziativa, però, sono i neolaureati e i neodottori di ricerca di diverse discipline che hanno voluto sottoporre il loro lavoro scientifico alla valutazione di questa commissione. Senza la loro disponibilità a contribuire alla discussione il dialogo sarebbe finito col ricevimento dei diplomi di laurea e/o PhD nelle diverse discipline. Ringrazio pertanto con molto affetto i giovani che hanno preso parte al Quinto Forum per Neolaureati.

Il frutto delle discussioni con i professori e tra i neolaureati nei singoli cluster è una scelta di articoli ben armonizzati tra loro: le piste di riflessione non terminano infatti coi singoli contributi ma procedono ben oltre per accompagnare il lettore verso un quadro più ampio. Questo ha implicato la necessità per ciascuno degli autori di rivedere il proprio lavoro da una nuova prospettiva disciplinare e di riscrivere i diversi articoli più volte. Purtroppo non tutti coloro che hanno

iniziato questo percorso nel gruppo sono riusciti a portarlo a compimento e si
sono ritirati da un procedimento impegnativo che, a conti fatti, è durato due
anni: è sempre un peccato perdere per strada persone che hanno contribuito in
maniera fondamentale alla discussione nei singoli cluster. Questo, tra l'altro, ha
comportato la necessità di rivedere le piste di riflessione nei singoli cluster, tuttavia auspico che l'esito qui presentato possa comunque contribuire alla discussione scientifica attuale e mi auguro che i lettori di questa raccolta di contributi,
compresi coloro che alla fine non vi hanno partecipato, trovino nei singoli contributi approcci interessanti, suggerimenti utili e forse anche nuovi orizzonti di
pensiero. Buona lettura, dunque, con la speranza che continuate a sostenere lo
spirito del forum per neolaureati!

Bibliographie

Somer, Murat/Tol, Gönül: "New Muslim Pluralism and Secular Democracy in
    Turkey and the EU". In: Prügl, Elisabeth/Thiel, Markus (eds.): *Diversity in the
    European Union*. Palgrave Macmillan: New York 2010, p. 96.
Stickings, Tim: '*They will only see Italy on a postcard': Italy's interior minister refuses
    to let rescue ship carrying 224 migrants dock, a week after turning away vessel
    with 630 people on board*. Daily Mail. Retrieved 28.06.2018, from: https://www.
    msn.com/en-ie/news/world/'they-will-only-see-italy-on-a-postcard'-italy's-
    interior-minister-refuses-to-let-rescue-ship-carrying-224-migrants-dock-a-
    week-after-turning-away-vessel-with-630-people-on-board/ar-AAz0cXo.

Inhaltsverzeichnis

I Transnational ties and movement

Dennis Fricken and Daniela Gruber

Introduction

This chapter contributes to the study of transnational space. The concept of transnationalism describes multiple connections and interactions between people or institutions linked to more than one nation state. Global changes and the increasing importance of transnational processes brought new challenges.

The Indian social and cultural anthropologist Arjun Appadurai describes transnational spaces as ethnoscapes, technoscapes, financescapes, mediascapes and ideoscapes and underlines their fluid structure: Scapes are composed by the perspective of different actors, such as national states, diaspora-communities and sub-national religious, political or economic communities, neighbours and individuals. Technoscapes refer to new technologies, which transcend rapidly national borders. Financescapes, according to Appadurai, describe global capital flows. All scapes have their own conditions and limitations; on the other hand, they determine the flow of the other scapes. Mediascapes and ideoscapes are described as landscapes of images, which are transported beyond national borders. Mediascapes transport real and also fictive images into the world, and ideoscapes are shared ideologies of states or counter-ideologies of movements. Tourists, refugees, asylum seekers, guest workers and other people and groups on the move build ethnoscapes[1].

Barth describes ethnic groups as one form of social organisation. Identity evolves from origin and social background. Actors use concepts of ethnic identity, to define themselves or others. Socially relevant factors determine the

---

1 Appadurai, Arjun: *Modernity at Large. Cultural Dimensions of Globalization.* Univ. of Minnesota Press, Minneapolis/London 1996/2010.

belonging to an ethnic group. As well as described in the chapter of Dennis Fricken, ethnic boundaries can refer to social and territorial basis. To maintain the own identity through the interaction with others is crucial for the expression of belonging and exclusion[2].

Pilgrims have an imaginary relationship to sacred centres. This effects on a religious belonging beyond long-distances. Through the creation of international networks by religious movements, global communities arise, to which individuals and groups can join. The participation of Roma and Sinti on international pilgrimages determines their belonging to a religious space, which transcends national boundaries. As Daniela Gruber's chapter shows, this may lead to tensions between religious universalities and local forms in a specific context.

The first chapter deals with conflicts and opportunities as a consequence of ethnic boundaries that come across whenever newcomers make their places in regions and locations that were used in a different manner before. Dennis Fricken describes the phenomenon of amenity migration and the related structural changes in the village of Oukaïmeden in the High Atlas in Morocco. Oukaïmeden can be characterized as a transnational space, which is used seasonally or periodically by mainly prosperous urban dwellers from Moroccan cities and foreign countries. On the basis of this type of in-migration, Oukaïmeden is a shared geographical place of the autochthonous group of Berbers on the one hand and newcomers on the other.

Daniela Gruber in the second contribution gives an insight in transnational religious space, by her study of transnational religious networks of Roma and Sinti in France and Austria. The Catholic Church has always acted beyond national boundaries. Under the centralistic leadership of Vatican, the Church creates and maintains transnational religious networks, grounded on a sense of belonging based on the Catholic faith. Roma and Sinti, who participate at international pilgrimages, can be considered as transnational actors. In her paper, Daniela Gruber examines in particular the influence of the Catholic Church on local Roma-communities in reflecting the construction of multiple identities.

Like the seasonal and periodic sojourners in Oukaïmeden, Roma and Sinti in France and Austria are also transnational actors who maintain different relations across nation states.

---

2   Barth, Frederik (Ed.): *Ethnic Groups and Boundaries: The Social Organization of Culture Difference.* Universitätsforlaget, Oslo 1970.

Referring to this volume "Cultures in dialogue", Dennis Fricken focuses on resulting conflicts between Berber communities and newcomers from increasing land usage and different world views in sharing Oukaïmeden place. In the second chapter, Daniela Gruber provides a critical view on cultural attributions to Sinti and Roma, linked to transnational religious networks within the pastoral care established by the Catholic Church.

References

Appadurai, Arjun: *Modernity at Large. Cultural Dimensions of Globalization.* Univ. of Minnesota Press, Minneapolis/London 1996/2010.
Barth, Frederik (Ed.): *Ethnic Groups and Boundaries: The Social Organization of Culture Difference.* Universitätsforlaget, Oslo 1970.

Dennis Fricken

Second residences in Oukaïmeden
Amenity migration in the High Atlas, Morocco

Abstract: Amenity migration, the seasonal or periodic movement of prosperous urban people into scenic rural areas, has its roots in the USA. In recent years, countries in the Global South have increasingly become the focus of amenity migration research. Oukaïmeden in Morocco is a village of particular interest, because the old Berber community at the upper limits of settlement in the High Atlas is known for the agrarian practices associated with traditional Berber culture. Beyond its spectacular setting and distinctive agricultural practices, the settlement geography of Oukaïmeden presents the observer with a striking settlement division: Berber houses and the second residences of, on the one hand, Arab Moroccans and, on the other, foreigners are located separated from each other. The presence of the amenity migrants leads to various structural changes. Due to the newcomers' various connections to their countries of origin, Oukaïmeden can be characterized as a transnational space.

1 Introduction

This chapter focuses on the phenomenon of amenity migration in Oukaïmeden, in the High Atlas region of Morocco. Amenity migration primarily describes the permanent, seasonal or periodic influx of mainly urban dwellers into a rural area, primarily due to the attractive scenery[1], while maintaining their main residence in their place of origin[2].

The phenomenon of amenity migration denotes a relatively young research field which has its roots in the USA[3]. After an increased number of studies in Europe, in particular the Alps, in recent years researchers have increasingly focused their attention on countries of the Global South[4]. In line with this

---

1   Moss, Laurence A. G.: "The Mountain Amenity Migration Phenomenon: Why it is happening and our response". In: Moss, Laurence A.G./Glorioso, Romella, S./Krause, Amy (eds.): *Understanding and Managing Amenity-Led Migration in Mountain Regions.* The Banff Centre: Banff 2009, pp. 1–12.
2   Moss, Laurence A. G. (ed.): *The Amenity Migrants: Seeking and Sustaining Mountains and Their Cultures.* CABI: Wallingford, UK 2006, p. 14.
3   Moss 2009, pp. 1–12.
4   Tonderayi, Desideria: "Amenity Migration and Tourism in the Eastern Highlands Bioregion of Zimbabwe: Policy, Planning and Management Considerations".

development, this chapter presents the first study about amenity migration in the Maghreb region of North Africa.

Located 80 km south of Marrakech, Oukaïmeden belongs to the administrative unit Marrakech-Tensift-El-Haouz. It is connected with Marrakech by two roads running through the plain El-Haouz. Oukaïmeden is an old Berber community at the upper settlement boundary in the High Atlas[5], where dwellings range up to an altitude of 2,754 m. It is the highest situated village in Morocco as well as a hotspot for winter sport tourism in the Maghreb. Oukaïmeden occupies an exposed location in a structurally weak mountainous region, known for the agrarian practices associated with traditional Berber culture. Beyond its spectacular setting and distinctive agricultural practices, the overall settlement geography of Oukaïmeden presents a visible dualistic structure. There is a striking settlement division: Berbers occupying the western half of the village, and the chalets or second residences of Arab Moroccans and foreigners prevalent in the north-east. The high mountain regions of the High Atlas were usually considered to be depopulation areas, Oukaïmeden is subject to demographic and socio-cultural change due to permanent, seasonal or periodic presence of amenity migrants.

Traditionally, the economy around Oukaïmeden consists of crop-related agriculture, combined with alternating grazing, where animals are moved between winter and summer pasturages. In this type of agriculture – also referred to as *transhumance* – the Imazigh Berbers typically take their goats and sheep to graze in the high valleys of the High Atlas during the summer[6,7]. During three months of pastoral farming in Oukaïmeden, shepherds dwell in the low stone and mud huts of the village. Thereafter, they return with the cattle to their families in the surrounding villages named *douar* (designation of typical Berber villages).

The purpose of the study was to figure out how Oukaïmeden is currently undergoing a socio-economic, demographic, cultural and settlement transformation

     In: Godde, Pamela et al. (eds.): *Tourism and Development in Mountain Regions*. CABI Publishing: Wallingford, UK 1999, pp. 297–322.
5   Steinicke, Ernst et al.: *Marokko. Eine geographische Exkursion*. Eigenverlag Universität Innsbruck: Innsbruck 2009, pp. 4–5.
6   Helfritz, Hans: *Berberburgen und Königsstädte des Islam: Ein Reisebegleiter zur Kunst Marokkos*. DuMont Schauberg: Köln 1986, pp. 67–69.
7   Breuer, Ingo: „Statistiken oder: Wie werden ‚Nomaden' in Marokko gemacht?". In: Gertel, Jörg (ed.): *Methoden als Aspekte der Wissenskonstruktion. Fallstudien zur Nomadismusforschung*. Mitteilungen des SFB "Differenz und Integration": Methoden als Aspekte der Wissenskonstruktion: Halle/Saale 2005, pp. 69–70.

in light of an increasingly prosperous urban Moroccan and foreign middle class, who transfer their second residences into the rural High Atlas region.

Amenity migration is more than a single unidirectional spatial movement. Detached from geographical separation, people commuting between regions of origin and regions of arrival introduce new ideas and lifestyle concepts. These interconnections are requirements for the development of a transnational space[8]. The newcomers add their own interpretations and meanings to relocate themselves to build up transnational connections. This study investigates whether recent developments indicate that Oukaïmeden became such a transnational space.

2 General methodological approach

This empirical research project combined different methods to analyse the phenomenon of amenity migration in Oukaïmeden. In addition to desktop and literature research and – in chronological order – data collection and analysis included expert interviews with Moroccan professors, a geographic mapping, standardized questionnaires and problem-focused interviews with Berbers in Oukaïmeden.

As a first step, the expert interviews with Professor Amrani Marrakchi (Department of Geography, University of Casablanca) and Professor Boujrouf (Department of Geography, University of Marrakech) were conducted to elaborate their understanding of the phenomenon of amenity migration. Applying qualitative content analysis method by Mayering (2000), the main goal was to order and structure the contents of communication and to develop a systemic textual analysis[9]. The interviews revealed that the development of second residences and influx of Moroccan and foreign newcomers are based on the fact that Oukaïmeden is a hotspot for winter sport tourism. Because of the recreational value and improved technical infrastructure, newcomers increasingly look for a periodic or seasonal sojourn in Oukaïmeden.

Moreover, my research stay in August and September 2012 included conducting a geographical mapping of the settlement structure and its functions

---

8   Pries, Ludger: „Transnationale Soziale Räume Theoretisch-empirische Skizze am Beispiel der Arbeitswanderungen Mexico – USA". *Zeitschrift für Soziologie* 25(6), 1996, p. 456.

9   Mayring, Philipp: "Qualitative Inhaltsanalyse". *Forum Qualitative Sozialforschung* 1(2) 2000.

in Oukaïmeden. The aim was to collect and analyse existing and planned spatial structures, land use and the use of buildings.

The next step was a semi-standardized survey of the Berber population as the basis to compare the attitudes and opinions on newcomers in Oukaïmeden. By means of a standardized questionnaire, a group of 19 Berbers were surveyed. The main topics included the perceptions of the newcomers, possible cultural conflicts, local interactions between Berbers and newcomers, and the significance of Oukaïmeden in the regional, national and international context.

Additionally, I applied problem-focused interviews in four home visits to Berbers. In Oukaïmeden, the objective was to figure out the individual perception of the situation regarding the topics demography, social and technical infrastructure, socio-economic situation, second residences and integration/conflict with newcomers. The four interviewed individuals are employed by newcomers as *gardeurs* (caretakers) in their second residences and hold a unique position: Unlike the group of 19 Berbers stated above, who are shepherds, owners of small general stores or restaurants and mobile vendors, a more intensive interaction between the group of newcomers and the group of caretakers was presumed. This part of the analysis was also based on qualitative content analysis by Mayering (2000)[10].

Some difficulties that occurred in the data collection were a result of the examination period. It became obvious that in summer, the owners of second homes are predominantly absent in Oukaïmeden. Due to this fact, the semi-standardized surveys of newcomers could not be executed because none of them was present during the time of research stay. Most newcomers stay for a longer period in wintertime for recreation and decentralized working.

Due to significant linguistic communication difficulties with the Berbers, who often spoke only the Berber dialect Tamazigh, a number of planned surveys in French had to be dropped.

3 Research results of amenity migration

As a result of diverse drivers, socio-economic dimensions and emerging challenges, amenity migration lead to various changes in the target location. This chapter gives an overview of these different drivers discussed in the relevant literature.

---

10 Mayring 2000.

The consequences of an increasing number of second residences in a community of rural character may be both positive and negative. Gosnell and Abrams (2011) showed that amenity migration may result in new jobs. These new jobs replace primary- and secondary-sector jobs in rural amenity areas. However, new jobs are likely to be highly seasonal, particularly in the case of high levels of absentee ownership[11]. At the same time, the increasing demand for real estate by wealthy migrants is likely to raise prices for land, real estate and housing, which frequently exceed the financial resources of the local population[12]. While infrastructure development as well as new institutional structures can often be beneficial, increasing population pressure may lead to a reduction of open spaces and a rise in negative environmental impacts (e.g. illegal dump sites, water pollution etc.)[13].

Besides the physical-geographical movement of newcomers into an amenity region, a social and identificatory change of location is observed. Global change, modern communication and transport technologies have a lasting effect on prerequisites, types and impacts of international migration. Transnational migration is characterized by the non-singular change between different places of residence in different states. It is a spreading of newcomers' social environment over national frontiers[14]. Based on this theory, amenity migration can be regarded as a part of transnational migration.

In consequence, conflicts stemming from cultural and behavioural differences often develop between the indigenous population and the newcomers. These cultural conflicts occur due to newcomers' specific imagination of life in rural regions[15]. Whereas the autochthonous population uses the target region for agricultural purposes, the main pull factors for newcomers are the scenic beauty, the leisure opportunities and the possibility to work site-independent, due to

---

11 Gosnell, Hannah/Abrams, Jesse: "Amenity Migration: Diverse Conceptualizations of Drivers, Socioeconomic Dimensions, and Emerging Challenges". *GeoJournal*, 76(4), 2011, p. 313.

12 Löffler, Roland/Steinicke, Ernst: "Counterurbanization and Its Socioeconomic Effects in High Mountain Areas of the Sierra Nevada (California/Nevada)". *Mountain Research and Development*, 26(1), 2006, p. 67.

13 Moss 2006, p. 9.

14 Pries, Ludger: "Transnationalismus, Migration und Inkorporation. Herausfordungen an Raum- und Sozialwissenschaften". *Geographische Revue*, 5(2), 2003, p. 29.

15 Boucquey, Noëlle et al.: "Interpreting Amenities, Envisioning the Future: Common Ground and Conflict in North Carolina's Rural Coastal Communities". *GeoJournal*, 77(1), 2012, p. 86.

an improved technical infrastructure[16]. Despite lacking experience of the rural life, the – generally prosperous – newcomers refuse to dispense their high urban standards and habits. Glorioso and Moss (2007) note the increasing influence of newcomers on regional structures, for example, modern and extensive shopping facilities or medical care[17]. As a result of these developments, tertiary-sector jobs gradually replace primary- and secondary-sector jobs[18].

The newcomers' request for seasonal or periodic shifting of their first (urban) and second (rural) residence as a form of multi-local living and working provoke not only economically and culturally structural changes but also settlement-geographical and ecological consequences[19]. The increasing land usage (e.g. construction of private and public buildings) and the consumption of energy as well as the expansion of traffic infrastructure may have negative effects on the often-fragile ecosystems[20].

4 Amenity migration in Oukaïmeden

In Morocco, one can observe the development of amenity migration destinations. Particularly, the majority of second homes are situated in popular urban tourist destinations such as Marrakech, Agadir and Essaouira[21]. This contrasts with amenity destinations in the Global North, where newcomers establish their second residence in rural regions[22]. In the expert interview, Amrani noted that in addition to the urban form of multi-local habitation, in recent years amenity migration was also established in Moroccan rural areas. A group of urban Moroccan amenity migrants relocate their second residence seasonally or periodically to Oukaïmeden[23]. Amrani further stated a major driving force behind

16 Moss 2006, p. 9.
17 Glorioso, Romella, S./Moss, Laurence, A. G.: "Amenity Migration to Mountain Regions: Current Knowledge and a Strategic Construct for Sustainable Management". *Social Change*, 37(1), 2007, p. 139.
18 Gosnell/Abrams, "Amenity Migration" 2011, p. 304.
19 McIntyre, Norman: "Multiple Dwelling and Managing Amenity-Led Migration in Mountain Regions". In: Moss, Laurence A. G. et al. (eds.): *Understanding and Managing Amenity-Led Migration in Mountain Regions*. Banff Centre Press: Banff 2009, p. 14.
20 Glorioso/Moss, "Amenity Migration" 2007, p. 140.
21 Interview Amrani, 2012.
22 Löffler, Roland/Steinicke, Ernst: „Counterurbanisierung in der kalifornischen Sierra Nevada. Das Hochgebirge als neuer Siedlungsraum". In: Innsbrucker Geographische Gesellschaft (ed.): *Innsbrucker Jahresbericht 2003-2007*. Innsbruck University Press: Innsbruck 2008, p. 44.
23 Interview Amrani, 2012.

this development was tourism. Due to the largest ski area in all the north of Africa, Oukaïmeden is a destination with high touristic potential. Subsequently, newcomers found existing structures in Oukaïmeden because the technical and traffic infrastructure was already available. As a result of both expert interviews with Amrani and Boujrouf, today Oukaïmeden and the adjacent Ourika Valley generally rank among the best-known and most popular mountain destinations for newcomers in Morocco[24,25].

Settlement geography

Owing to geographical mapping, the strictly spatial differentiation of the village was evident: The northeast hill of Oukaïmeden is populated only by amenity residents (Fig. 1). In recent years, this area was equipped with technical devices for telecommunications, with reliable electricity and water supply, and with a paved road network. The Berber *douar* on the western hill have no access to this modern infrastructure.

It is striking that despite good transportation links and modern technical infrastructure, facilities such as major shopping centres, medical clinics and schools are non-existent. Although their absence is noted by native Berbers in conversation, sometimes even criticized, they consider their centre of life to be with their families in the surrounding villages. For newcomers, seasonal schools are not necessary. The limited range of shopping opportunities can be explained by the fact that tourists are adequately supplied in hotels, while newcomers usually bring supplies from their home areas. As a reaction to the higher demands of tourists and amenity migrants, a little medical ward is established in Oukaïmeden during winter season.

The investigation shows a homogeneous and dualistic view of Oukaïmeden. Built as a traditional Berber-*douar*, a new district in Oukaïmeden was developed by the presence of newcomers (Fig. 1).

Socio-cultural dimension

In some discussions with the expert interviewees and the Berbers, they emphasized the increasing importance of international visitors and migrants. This was confirmed in the conducted expert interviews in Oukaïmeden: Both groups (professors and Berbers) pointed to the influx of amenity migrants from Europe

---

24 Interview Amrani, 2012.
25 Interview Boujrouf, 2012.

Oukaimeden

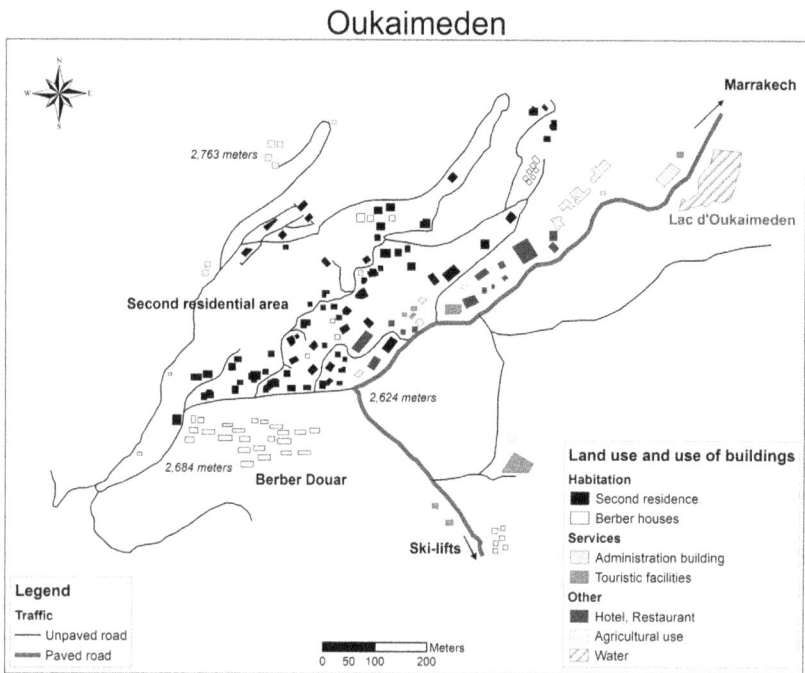

Fig. 1: Use of buildings in Oukaïmeden (own mapping)

(especially from France, England, Italy and Spain). Especially French residents are of importance: They are often French Moroccans who are second-generation emigrants to France and who acquire second or even third residences in the country of their parents. Frequently, these newcomers of foreign origin are motivated to contribute to the development of their home country[26].

Amrani noticed the difference between national (Moroccan) and international (European) newcomers in Oukaïmeden: In Morocco, the gap between rich and poor is more pronounced than in Europe. As part of the Moroccan Bourgeoise, the owners of the chalets in Oukaïmeden are prosperous and

---

26 Ait Mous, Fadma: „Marocanité: Identitäten und Chatrooms der Diaspora". In: Gertel, Jörg/Breuer, Ingo (eds.): *Alltagsmobilitäten. Aufbruch marokkanischer Lebenswelten.* Transcript Verlag: Bielefeld 2012, p. 400.

economically independent. As a result, they do not need their second residences for mobile working to increase their income[27].

Like amenity migrants in the countries of the Global North, potential owners of second homes in Morocco are looking for a location with a low crime rate. Due to its remoteness, in Oukaïmeden they find a peaceful location, privacy and high recreational value. The newcomers come out of their well-equipped urban homes to Oukaïmeden, where they create their own microcosm. Unlike in the Rocky Mountains or the Alps[28,29] in which the cultural background of an amenity destination represents a significant pull factor for newcomers (who often adopt this new, rural way of life and modify into a new form in accordance with their imagination of rural life), this phenomenon does not exist in Oukaïmeden. Berber culture may be interesting for several migrants, but most migrants do not adopt the Berber lifestyle which is visible in Oukaïmeden in pasturing.

Cultural differences are both distinct and observable. Based on different socio-economic backgrounds, two thirds of the Berbers stated that cultural differences arrive with newcomers. Cultural barriers exist between the two groups. Due to this fact and the different times of the year Berbers and newcomers spend in Oukaïmeden, there is no in-depth interaction between traditional-living Berbers and urban, sometimes Westernized Arab immigrants or foreigners. In addition, a deficient knowledge of French and Arab languages of predominant Tamazigh-speaking Berbers is observed. By contrast, the Arabic-speaking Moroccans and foreigners do not speak Berber dialect.

As a result, reinforcing interactions between Berbers and amenity migrants are almost exclusively limited to the *gardeur* (caretaker) relationship. Berbers working as ski sport employees in winter may instruct newcomers, but tourists are their main target. Berber street vendors and restaurants are frequented primarily by day-trippers and longer-remaining tourists. Thus, points of social contact are almost non-existent. Berbers and newcomers in Oukaïmeden live largely separated from one another, resulting in a village characterized by both traditional and late-modern lifestyles.

Some locals reacted with surprise when being asked to what extent they feel newcomers are integrated into local society. Most of them made no comment. As mentioned in the relevant literature of Moss (2006)[30] or Gosnell and Abrams

---

27 Interview Amrani, 2012.
28 Moss, 2006, p. 11.
29 Löffler & Steinicke, 2006, p. 69.
30 Moss, 2006.

$(2011)^{31}$, newcomers gain influence on municipal structures, institution-building and the cultural identity of the community. By contrast, this is not the case in Oukaïmeden. Due to the dualistic settlement structure and spatial segregation as shown in Fig. 1, Oukaïmeden can be described as a culturally heterogeneous village in which – depending on the season – user groups of different influence reside. Newcomers keep largely to themselves and build up transnational networks among themselves.

In the article of Gruber (published in this chapter), the author pointed out that transnational networks arise through new possibilities in communication and transport and by people on the move[32]. In addition to these considerations, in Oukaïmeden connections between newcomers' place of origin and the target region are based on the settlement geographical and socio-cultural dimensions as stated above.

Demographic dimension

Amenity migration in Oukaïmeden differs significantly from the type documented in well-known amenity destinations in North America and Europe as noted by Gosnell and Abrams (2011)[33] and Steinicke (2007)[34]. Since the Berbers practise transhumance, they reside for only two to three summer months in the village. In spring, they traditionally do not drive their cattle to the high pastures, allowing nature time for regeneration. During summer, the owners of second homes come to Oukaïmeden for weekend getaways. Longer stays only occur during the winter season, from November to March, a period when the majority of Berbers live with their families in the surrounding villages[35]. Thus, the population of Oukaïmeden fluctuates steadily throughout the different seasons of the year. Only approximately 50 people – some restaurant owners, mobile vendors, owners of small general stores and the military stationed there – are present permanently on site. The expert interviews revealed a winter population of

31 Gosnell & Abrams, 2011.
32 Smith, Michael Peter/Guarnizo, Luis: "The Locations of Transnationalism". In: Smith, Michael Peter/Guarnizo, Luis (eds): *Transnationalism from Below*. Transaction Publishers: New Brunswick/London 1998, p. 4.
33 Gosnell/Abrams, "Amenity Migration" 2011.
34 Steinicke, Ernst: „Amenity Migration: Die neuen Bewohner der Alpen. Skizze eines Forschungsprojektes". In: Innsbrucker Geographische Gesellschaft (ed.). *Alpine Kulturlandschaft im Wandel. Hugo Penz zum 65, Geburtstag*. Innsbruck University Press: Innsbruck, 2007, pp. 213–225.
35 Interview Amrani, 2012.

450–600 predominant newcomers. In summer, the population density is much lower. As a consequence of a dwindling Berber pastoral system in the High Atlas, the number of inhabitants has been declining steadily for decades. Today the village consists of 50–150 summer residents: The number includes around 40 male Berber shepherds, some of their family members from the Ourika Valley and surrounding villages, restaurant owners, mobile vendors, owners of small general stores and the military. In exceptional cases, the presence of isolated newcomers is possible.

In addition to those Berbers residing during summertime and newcomers using their second homes seasonally or periodically in winter, another type of resident can be identified in Oukaïmeden: tourists as temporary visitors who spend their holidays especially in winter for up to two weeks in the village.

Economic dimension

As noted by Amrani and Boujrouf, several different groups simultaneously reside in Oukaïmeden. They enable Berbers from surrounding villages various income opportunities: Some Berbers are employed as *gardeurs* (caretakers) for owners of second homes. They monitor and maintain the chalets of amenity migrants during their absence. In return, chalet owners usually provide caretakers with a small accommodation that is connected directly to the chalet. Besides free access to electricity and water, the average wages for a caretaker is about 500 Moroccan dirhams (about 50 euros) per month[36,37]. Since this is hardly a salary level sufficient for neither the caretakers themselves nor their families in the surrounding *douars,* caretakers usually work for two or more owners of second residences. Some Berbers obtain additional income as guides for hiking tours in the summer, in ski equipment rental and skiing instructors in winter. Based on the theory of Gosnell and Abrams (2011) and due to the increasing tertiarisation, jobs of the tertiary sector replace gradually those of the primary and secondary sector in Oukaïmeden. The demands of transnational amenity migrants are significant drivers of this development.

In accordance with expert interviews, real estate and land prices have risen in recent years due to the influx of wealthy urban dwellers. The Berbers, however, do not necessarily consider this as negative, because they purchase no construction land in Oukaïmeden. For generations, the simple *douar* on the western hills have been adequate for their needs.

---

36 Interview Amrani, 2012.
37 Interview Boujrouf, 2012.

5 Synthesis

In recent years Oukaïmeden has been developed on several levels, by the establishment of second homes purchased by wealthy Moroccans and Europeans.
The original character of Oukaïmeden – founded by Berbers as a seasonal
residence for pasture grazing in summer – has changed significantly: The
increase of second residences requires an expansion of first-rate technical and
traffic infrastructure that newcomers are used to from their urban homes in
Morocco or Europe. The technical progress, especially modern communication and transport technologies, enhances Oukaïmeden as a target region for
transnational migration. The newcomers with roots in Morocco and Europe
change their residence in periodical intervals between Oukaïmeden and their
state of origin.

   Oukaïmeden distinguishes itself fundamentally from amenity migration
destinations in North America and Europe. Language barriers between local
Berbers and newcomers are substantial. A limited cultural dialogue takes
place between Berbers and Arab Moroccan/foreign newcomers: Contacts
between these two groups are apparent only in the employment situations
of the caretakers. Due to this limited interaction, and because Berbers and
newcomers occupy the village at different seasons, no serious cross-cultural
conflicts seem to have emerged. No distinct lifestyle is imposed upon the
Berbers through the presence of amenity migrants, as the two groups largely
ignore one another.

   Oukaïmeden can be characterized as a place with transnational influences
by different groups of urban dwellers from Morocco itself and from various
European states. Newcomers bring their own lifestyle, leisure activities and
comfort- and equipment requirements to the village. Winter activities like
skiing require technical infrastructure. For using their second residences as
a seasonal working base, an adequate quality of electricity and internet as
well as a permanent supply of clean drinking water is necessary. In order to
meet the demands of the newcomers, the idea emerged to build a mosque in
Oukaïmeden.

   Finally, amenity migration as a part of transnational migration implies an
increase of socio-cultural diversity in Oukaïmeden. The different presences of
Berbers and newcomers in Oukaïmeden, the traditional Berber culture and
the late-modern lifestyle of sometimes Westernized Arab immigrants as well as
three different languages (Tamazigh, French and Arab) lead to Oukaïmedens'
culturally inhomogeneity.

References

Ait Mous, Fadma: „Marocanité: Identitäten und Chatrooms der Diaspora". In: Gertel, Jörg/Breuer, Ingo (Hgs.): *Alltagsmobilitäten. Aufbruch marokkanischer Lebenswelten.* Transcript Verlag: Bielefeld 2012, pp. 389–404.

Boucquey, Noëlle et al.: "Interpreting amenities, envisioning the future: common ground and conflict in North Carolina's rural coastal communities". *GeoJournal*, 77(1), 2012, pp. 83–101.

Breuer, Ingo: „Statistiken oder: Wie werden "Nomaden" in Marokko gemacht?". In: Gertel, Jörg (Hg.): *Methoden als Aspekte der Wissenskonstruktion. Fallstudien zur Nomadismusforschung.* Mitteilungen des SFB "Differenz und Integration": Methoden als Aspekte der Wissenskonstruktion. Orientwiss. Zentrum der Martin-Luther-Univ. Halle-Wittenberg: Halle/Saale 2005, pp. 55–73.

Glorioso, Romella S./Moss, Laurence A. G.: "Amenity migration to mountain regions: current knowledge and a strategic construct for sustainable management". *Social Change*, 37(1), 2007, pp. 137–161.

Gosnell, Hannah/Abrams, Jesse: "Amenity migration: diverse conceptualizations of drivers, socioeconomic dimensions, and emerging challenges". *GeoJournal*, 76(4), 2011, pp. 303–322.

Helfritz, Hans: *Berberburgen und Königstädte des Islam: Ein Reisebegleiter zur Kunst Marokkos*, DuMont Schauberg: Köln 1986.

Löffler, Roland/Steinicke, Ernst: "Counterurbanization and its socioeconomic effects in high mountain areas of the Sierra Nevada (California/Nevada)". *Mountain Research and Development*, 26(1), 2006, pp. 64–71.

Löffler, Roland/Steinicke, Ernst: "Counterurbanisierung der kalifornischen Sierra Nevada. Das Hochgebirge als neuer Siedlungsraum". In: Innsbrucker Geographische Gesellschaft (Hg.): *Innsbrucker Jahresbericht 2003–2007.* Innsbruck University Press: Innsbruck 2008, pp. 43–59.

Mayring, Philipp: "Qualitative Inhaltsanalyse". *Forum Qualitative Sozialforschung*, 1(2), 2000.

McIntyre, Norman: "Multiple Dwelling and Managing Amenity-Led Migration in Mountain Regions". In: Moss, Laurence A. G. et al. (eds.) *Understanding and Managing Amenity-led Migration in Mountain Regions. Proceedings of the Mountain Culture at the Banff Centre conference held May 15–19, 2008.* Banff Centre Press: Banff 2009, pp. 13–22.

Moss, Laurence A. G. (ed.): *The Amenity Migrants: Seeking and Sustaining Mountains and Their Cultures*, CABI: Wallingford 2006.

Moss, Laurence A. G.: "The Mountain Amenity Migration Phenomenon: Why It Is Happening and Our Response". In: Moss, Laurence A.G./Glorioso, Romella

S./Krause, Amy. (eds.): *Understanding and Managing Amenity-Led Migration in Mountain Regions*. The Banff Centre: Banff 2009, pp. 1–12.

Pries, Ludger: „Transnationale Soziale Räume Theoretisch-empirische Skizze am Beispiel der Arbeitswanderungen Mexico – USA". *Zeitschrift für Soziologie*, 25(6), 1996, pp. 456–472.

Pries, Ludger: „Transnationalismus, Migration und Inkorporation. Herausforderungen an Raum- und Sozialwissenschaften". *Geographische Revue*, 5(2), 2003, pp. 23–40.

Smith, Michael Peter/Guarnizo, Luis: "The Locations of Transnationalism". In: Smith, Michael Peter/Guarnizo, Luis (eds.): *Transnationalism from Below*. Transaction Publishers: New Brunswick/London 1998, pp. 3–34.

Steinicke, Ernst: „Amenity Migration: Die neuen Bewohner der Alpen. Skizze eines Forschungsprojektes". In: Innsbrucker Geographische Gesellschaft (ed.): *Alpine Kulturlandschaft im Wandel. Hugo Penz zum 65, Geburtstag*. Innsbrucker Geographische Gesellschaft: Innsbruck 2007, pp. 213–225.

Steinicke, Ernst et al.: „*Marokko. Eine geographische Exkursion*". Eigenverlag Universität Innsbruck: Innsbruck 2009.

Tonderayi, Desideria: "Amenity Migration and Tourism in the Eastern Highlands Bioregion of Zimbabwe: Policy, Planning and Management Considerations". In: Godde, Pamela et al. (eds.): *Tourism and Development in Mountain Regions*. CABI Publishing: Wallingford 1999, pp. 297–322.

Interviews

Amrani, Mamoune M. (05/09/2012).
Boujrouf, Said (18/09/2012).

Daniela Gruber

Transnational religious networks of Roma and Sinti in France and Austria

Abstract: This chapter deals with the Catholic Church as a transnational religious move-ment and its impact on local communities of Sinti and Roma in France and Austria. Transnational religious movements, such as the Catholic Church, are connected at the organisational level beyond national boundaries. The specific pastoral care for Roma and Sinti is mainly grounded on their provided "otherness" and their marginalisation regarding the majority population. Local and international pilgrimages have a special significance for the creation of religious networks. They foster participation for Roma and Sinti and improve their relationships with the majority population.

1 Introduction

This article examines transnational religious networks of Roma and Sinti[1] in France and Austria. In my empirical study of two pilgrimages, which are dedi-cated to Roma and Sinti, the focus lies on the special position of Roma and Sinti within the Catholic Church and the influence of the Catholic Church as a trans-national religious movement on local communities of Sinti and Roma. I worked out how Roma, Sinti and priests shape religious networks, connected with mul-tiple identity constructions.

---

1 Roma is the self-denomination of some groups and the international term for several groups, such as the Cale, Sinti, Kalderasch, Lowari. Heuß, Herbert: „Die Migration von Roma aus Osteuropa im 19. und 20. Jahrhundert. Historische Anlässe und staatliche Reaktion – Überlegungen zum Funktionswechsel des Zigeuner-Ressentiments." In: Giere, Jacqueline: *Die gesellschaftliche Konstruktion des Zigeuners: Zur Genese eines Vorurteils.* Campus Verlag: Frankfurt/New York 1996b, pp. 109 f. The unity of Roma results mainly from their marginalisation regarding the majority population. Barany, Zoltan: *The East European Gypsies: Regime, Change, Marginality, and Ethnopolitics.* Cambridge Univ. Press 2002, p. 2. Today Roma and Sinti on an international level are classified as migrants, migrant workers, refugees, asylum seekers or displaced or state-less people. Liégeois, Jean Pierre: *Roma in Europe.* Council of Europe 2007, pp. 25, 31.

2 Research fields and methods

My research fields were the annual pilgrimages in Saintes Maries de la Mer in France and Mariazell in Austria. The methodological approach comprises a qualitative study of the two pilgrimages from 2008 to 2012. The collection of empirical data occurred in the survey of religious networks[2] through qualitative interviews and participant observation. For the interviews with participating Roma, Sinti and priests, I prepared an interview guideline[3]. I analysed the collected data by using the thematic coding procedure according to Flick[4], which is a modification of the procedure of grounded theory developed by Glaser and Strauss[5].

During my fieldwork, I conducted fourteen interviews and informal talks with Roma, Sinti and priests in France and Austria. With Sinti and Roma, I talked about their personal faith, their relation to the Catholic Church and how important pilgrimages are for them. The interviews with priests focused on their work with Roma. Through these interviews, I also received information about network relationships in addition to the pilgrimages, in the local parishes. The data from participant observation had been collected in Saintes Maries de la Mer in the years 2008, 2009 and 2010, and in Mariazell in 2008 and 2011.

Every year around May 24th, 30.000 Sinti and Roma from different European countries meet at Saintes Maries de la Mer in France to celebrate for one week during pilgrimage. The highlight of the pilgrimage is the procession of Sainte

2 Mitchell, J.C. (Ed.): *Social Networks in Urban Situations*. University Press: Manchester 1969, pp. 2–5. Jansen, Dorothea: *Einführung in die Netzwerkanalyse*. Leske und Buderich: Opladen 2003, pp. 70–163. Schenk, Michael: *Soziale Netzwerke und Kommunikation*. (Habilitationsschrift der Wirtschafts- und Sozialwissenschaftlichen Fakultät der Universität Augsburg) Mohr: Tübingen 1984, pp. 3–77. Schnegg, Michael/ Lang, Hartmut (Eds.): „Netzwerkanalyse. Eine praxisorientierte Einführung. " *Methoden der Ehnographie* Heft 1 2002, pp. 1–27.
3 Schlehe, Judith: „Formen qualitativer ethnografischer Interviews." In: Beer, Bettina (Ed.): *Methoden und Techniken der Feldforschung*. Dietrich Reimer Verlag: Berlin 2003, pp. 78 f. Schmidt, Christiane: „Analyse von Leitfadeninterviews." In: Flick Uwe/Von Kardoff Ernst/Steinke Ines (Hrsg.): *Qualitative Forschung. Ein Handbuch*. Rowohlt Taschenbuch Verlag: Reinbek bei Hamburg 2000/2007, pp. 447–452.
4 Flick, Uwe: *Qualitative Sozialforschung: Eine Einführung*. Rowohlt Taschenbuch Verlag: Hamburg 2002, pp. 272–277.
5 Strauss, A.L.: *Grundlagen qualitativer Sozialforschung: Datenanalyse und Theoriebildung in der empirischen soziologischen Forschung*. Fink: München 1991. Glaser, Barney G/Strauss, Anselm L.: *The Discovery of Grounded Theory: Strategies for Qualitative Research*. Aldine Transaction Publishers: New Brunswick/London 2009.

Sara on May 24th, the Roma's patron saint. In the crypt below the church are preserved the relics of Sainte Sara. During the days of pilgrimage, the door of the crypt is open, and pilgrims make offerings to the statue of Sara. Parents bring their children to be baptised in the Church of Saintes Maries de la Mer. Every evening there are masses with different topics. Roma and Sinti are involved in the organisation of these masses. At the day of procession on 24th, the relics of Sara are lowered down from the altar in the church and Roma and Sinti carry the statue of Sara from the church to the sea. When the procession arrives at the sea, they let the relics symbolically sink into the sea. Pilgrims and many tourists, who wish to visit and experience this special ritual, gather at the beach of Saintes Maries de la Mer. There are two legends to which this ritual is related. One legend describes Sara, the Egyptian servant of Maria Salomä and Maria Jakobäa, after her escape from persecution of Christians in the Holy Land, stranded at the mouth of the river Rhône in the Camargue. From there they began to convert the local population. According to another legend, Sara was a Romnia, a Gitana, who rescued the two Maries from the stormy sea[6].

The pilgrimage in Mariazell in Austria is held every year on August 15th, the day of "Maria Himmelfahrt". As in France, Roma and Sinti participated at the pilgrimage already in pre-war time. Mariazell has been a place of pilgrimage for centuries. The monk Magnus brought the Maria's wood figurine in 1157 to Mariazell. He constructed a chapel and his hermitage today builds the centre of the basilica[7]. In 2011 around eighty to hundred Sinti and Roma participated at the pilgrimage. They came from Austria, Germany and Slovenia. The mass was held in German, but parts of the mass were also in Romanes, the language of some groups[8]. After mass, Roma, Sinti and priests had lunch together and, in the afternoon, they organised a small celebration with music as part of a cultural afternoon.

During my fieldwork, I attended the masses and rituals at both pilgrimages. I participated during the pilgrimage week at the festivities around the church and at the caravan space in Saintes Maries de la Mer and stayed there for several

6   Vossen, Rüdiger: *Roma, Sinti, Gitanos, Gypsies: Zwischen Verfolgung und Romantisierung.* Katalog zur Ausstellung des Hamburgischen Museums für Völkerkunde: Frankfurt a. M./Berlin/Wien 1983, pp. 229 ff.

7   Mayer, Daniela: "Holy Mother Mary, Pray for Us Sinners – Catholic Pilgrimage in Austria." In: Shahshahani, Soheila (Ed.): *Cities of Pilgrimage.* Lit: Berlin 2009, pp. 127–134.

8   Heinschink, Mozes F./Hemetek, Ursula (Eds.): *Roma: Das unbekannte Volk. Schicksal und Kultur.* Böhlau Verlag: Wien/Köln/Weimar 1994, pp. 114 f.

days. With some Roma and pastoral workers, I travelled to Mariazell by bus, organised by the Romano Centro in Vienna. We had lunch at a restaurant and we spent the afternoon together.

3 Transnational religious movements

The theoretical background of my research is grounded in concepts of transnational religious movements. Transnational religion refers to every religious system, which transcends national boundaries at the organisational level[9]. The issues in this context, which are based on my study, contain particularly the formation of religious networks, transformations of religious practices and ideas connected with multiple identity constructions[10], as well as the production of religious places in a globalised world[11].

Religious movements such as the Catholic Church have always acted across national borders. Missionaries brought the Christian faith into the world. Through the idea of homogenisation and the global connection by local churches, universal identities arise, which are grounded in the Catholic faith.[12] The Roman

---

9   Hervieu-Léger, Danièle: "Faces of Catholic Transnationalism. In and Beyond France." In: Hoeber Rudolph Susanne/Piscatori, James (Eds.): *Transnational Religion and Fading States*. Westview Press: Colorado/Oxford 1997, p. 104.

10 Coleman, Simon/Collins, Peter: *Religion, Identity and Change. Perspectives on Global Transformations*. MPG Books: Cornwall 2004, pp. 3–8. Six-Hohenbalken, Maria Anna: „Religionen in Bewegung." In: Six-Hohenbalken Maria Anna/Tosic Jelena (Eds.): *Anthropologie der Migration: Theoretische Grundlagen und interdisziplinäre Aspekte*. Fakultas: Wien 2009, pp. 256 f.

11 Levitt, Peggy: *Between God, Ethnicity, and Country: An Approach to the Study of Transnational Religion*. Paper presented at workshop on "Transnational Migration: Comparative Perspectives", June 30–July 1, Princeton University 2001. Retrieved 14.05.2012, from: http://www.transcomm.ox.ac.uk/working%20papers/Levitt.pdf.
    Van der Veer, Peter: *Nation and Religion: Perspectives on Europe and Asia*. Princeton Univ. Press 1999. Van der Veer, Peter: *Transnational Religion*. Paper given to the conference on Transnational Migration: Comparative Perspectives. Princeton University, 30 June–1 July 2001. Retrieved 14.05.2012, from: http://www.transcom.ox.ac.uk/working%20papers/WPTC-0118%20Van%der%20Veer.pdf.Vertovec, Steven: *Religion and Diaspora*. Paper presented at the conference on "New Landscapes of Religion in the West", Scool of Geography and the Environment, University of Oxford, 27–29 September 2000. Retrieved 14.05.2012, from: http://www.transcomm.ox.ac.uk/working%20papers/Vertovec01PDF.Vertovec, Steven: *Transnationalism*. Routledge: New York 2010.

12 Idem, p. 1.

Catholicism as a transnational religious movement creates and maintains a network of ideologically unified communities, linked to the central government of the Vatican. On the one hand, a religious pluralism developed within the church itself, and on the other hand the church tries to enforce and strengthen the uniformity in claiming dominance and power[13].

In contrast to focusing on religious institutions as global actors, the concept of *transnationalism from below*[14] according to Smith and Guarnizo emphasises religious activities of individuals and groups regarding their transnational relationships based on a shared ideology. Smith and Guarnizo describe "transnationalism from below" as "spaces", which result from transnational migration and related cultural hybridity. Therefore, they use transnationalism as a concept that presents phenomena, which are not new, but gained a new intensity within the global context in the 20th century.

Transnational networks arise through new possibilities in communication and transport, by people on the move, family ties and religious ideologies. Multiple social ties are grounded on the level of family, economy, social issues, religion and policies. In this way, networks emerge across one or more nation states and across ethnic boundaries.

The concept of transnationalism describes multiple connections and interactions. People or institutions are connected beyond nation states. Of particular importance in regard to economic, social and political connections between people, places and institutions are transnational relationships between social groups. Ethnic groups, religious movements and political organisations increasingly transcend specific territorial boundaries and identities.

Appadurai uses the term *ethnoscapes* to describe altered conditions of the social, territorial and cultural reproduction of group identity. Ethnoscapes comprise landscapes of people such as tourists, refugees, asylum-seekers, guest workers and other groups and individuals on the move. There are no longer territorial separated groups based on family ties, such as in traditional

---

13 Hervieu-Léger, Danièle: "Faces of Catholic Transnationalism. In and Beyond France." In: Hoeber Rudolph Susanne/Piscatori, James (Eds.): *Transnational Religion and Fading States.* Westview Press: Colorado/Oxford 1997, pp. 104–106. Casanova, José: "Globalizing Catholicism and the Return to a Universal Church". In: Hoeber Rudolph/Piscatori (Eds.), 1997, p. 134. Kurtz, Lester R.: *Gods in the Global Village.* Pine Forge Press: Thousand Oaks 1995.

14 Smith, Michael Peter/Guarnizo, Luis (Eds.): *Transnationalism from Below: Comparative Urban and Community Research. Volume 6.* Transaction Publishers: New Brunswick/London 1998.

anthropology research, but they are culturally inhomogeneous, and the geographical boundaries are fluid[15].

Peggy Levitt states that studies on transnational religious practices ideally
include all aspects of religious life. In this way, it can be shown how people as
transnational actors use religious symbols and ideas for the construction of multiple identities.[16] However, religion should not be seen equal to identity. There
are several reasons for the commitment to a religious group or ideology. The
elements, which are contained in religious practices and rituals, are only in part
tied up with identity. Also, other factors such as class and gender contribute significantly to its formation[17]. Religious identities are not static, but rather they
are in permanent transformation and are permanently negotiated[18]. Due to the
expansion of religious networks, multiple identities arise, which transcend the
borders of nation states.

In former times, international trade, conquest and colonisation fostered the
expansion of religions. The new transnationalism is often represented by "religion from below"[19], by popular religion, everyday religiosity and the religion of
"the poor and oppressed", more than indoctrinated from above.

4 Roma and Sinti in the Catholic Church

Global religious movements are based on a homogenised form of admiration,
while local practices can take different forms. The Catholic Church creates a
global community to which local communities and individuals of Roma and
Sinti can join. The local churches are connected and Catholic Roma and Sinti
are part of the parish in their surroundings. The Church considers Roma and
Sinti as a particular minority and issues recommendations for a specific pastoral program. It is grounded mainly on their provided "otherness" and their
marginalisation with regard to the major population[20].

---

15 Appadurai, Arjun: *Modernity at Large: Cultural Dimensions of Globalization*. Univ. of
    Minnesota Press: Minneapolis/London 2010, p. 48.
16 Levitt, 2001, pp. 8, 9.
17 Coleman/Collins, 2004, pp. 3–8.
18 Six-Hohenbalken, 2009, pp. 256 f.
19 Hoeber Rudolph/Piscatori, 1997, p. 3.
20 In France, after the Second World War, padre Fleury and a group of priests established
    the pastoral care for Roma and Sinti. Already during war, some priests had access to
    arrested Roma and Sinti in the concentration camps in France for providing spiritual
    aid. Retrieved, 08.06.2012, from: http://memoires-tsiganes1939-1946.fr/.

Local and international pilgrimages, which are dedicated to Roma and Sinti, take on significant importance in creating religious networks. Pilgrims develop a common relationship to religious centres. This creates and also connects imaginary relations and senses of belonging over long distances. As Peggy Levitt states: "Religious icons and sacred shrines, rather than national flags, proclaim these religious spaces"[21]. Through participation at the pilgrimages, Roma and Sinti are part of a religious space, which transcends national borders.

New developments show that Roma and Sinti are more involved at the pilgrimages and in the local parishes. In a detailed study on the pilgrimage in Saintes Maries de la Mer in 1975, Greverus[22] describes that Roma and Sinti were a minority of the participants at the evening masses. The focus at these masses was on the person of Jesus Christ. Sara did not matter; she was not even recognised as a saint by the Catholic Church until 2000[23].

One reason for the Church's efforts for a greater inclusion of Roma and Sinti, can also be found in their numerous conversions to the Pentecostal churches in the last fifty years. As members of the Pentecostal church, Roma and Sinti began to become priests themselves. This role often leads to higher power and influence, linked to a transformation of socio-political relationships[24].

In Saintes Maries de la Mer priests and deacons from Roma communities increasingly participate at the pilgrimage. The bishops in France issue so-called safe conducts to Roma and Sinti, which enable them to also undertake religious services in their communities. The consecrations of Roma as priests are new developments in France. In Austria this is not yet the case, but there is also the aim of an intern spiritual welfare within Roma communities. The diocese in Burgenland, Austria, for instance, works together with a member of the Roma

---

21 Levitt, 2001, p. 20.
22 Greverus, Ina Maria: *Zigeuner und wir.* Institut für Kulturanthropologie und Europäische Ethnologie der Johann Wolfgang Goethe-Universität: Frankfurt 1975.
23 The data originate from a timetable at the exhibition of the "Société des Saintes Maries de la Mer" in May 2011.
24 Cantón Delgado, Manuela: *Croyances protestantes: Stratégies Gitanes.* Religions revisitées Revue trimestrielle numéro 20, 2004, pp. 88–106. Gay y Blasco, Paloma: *Gitano Evangelism: The Emergence of a Politico-Religious Diaspora.* Paper presented at the 6th EASA Conference, Krakow 26–29 July. Retrieved 14.05.2012, from: https://transcomm. ox.ac.uk/working%20papers/WPTC-01-04%20Gayyblasco.pdf.
Kücher, Gertraud: *Fahrende Roma und Sinti in Österreich im beginnenden 21. Jahrhundert. Eine Untersuchung sozialanthropologischer Theorieansätze ausgehend vom Rastplatz für fahrende Roma und Sinti in Braunau am Inn.* (Diplomarbeit) Wien 2006.

group from the settlement in Oberwart[25]. He is engaged in his community for
spiritual care, and he also participates in the organisation of the pilgrimage in
Mariazell.

4.1 Reproducing stereotypes and homogeneous concepts of identity

The Catholic Church postulates a universal validity and creates homogeneous
identities, based on the Catholic faith, and with clear ideas of what "being a
good Christian" means. The fact that some Roma are baptised, but do not participate at the mass, only at the pilgrimages, is seen by the Church as not sufficient. Consequently, the Church requests a stronger missionary work, to push
them forward to the "right faith". For this reason, the Church instructs pastors
who live in Roma communities. In this way Roma and Sinti should deepen the
Christian faith.

In the official document of the Vatican[26], which contains recommendations
for the Roma-pastoral, the Catholic Church tends to reproduce stereotypes and
homogeneous concepts of identity with which Roma and Sinti had to struggle
since their arrival in Europe[27]. The Catholic Church does not agree with some
"cultural aspects", which do not correspond to Christian values. In particular, the
Church refers to women's status and work attitudes, as well as their relation to the
major population, emphasising also their apparently "deeply rooted otherness".
Although the question of the legitimacy of such statements arises, the Catholic
Church creates cultural assumptions, which should confirm their alterity, and
in consequence, the Church emphasises the need for stronger missionary work.

The Catholic Church in the official paper of the Vatican and at the pilgrimage
in France accentuates strongly the Roma's peripatetic life, but today only two
per cent of Roma and Sinti are living a peripatetic way of life[28]. Even though the

25 Retrieved 03.07.2017, from: http://www.burgenland-roma.at/index.php/geschichte/
    das-attentat.
26 The Vatican in the journal "People on the Move" Nr. 100 published the document in
    2005 with recommendations for the Pastoral Care of Migrants and Itinerant Groups.
    Retrieved 26.04.2012, from: http://www.vatikan.va/roman_curia/pontifical_councils/
    migrants/documents/rc_pc_migrants_doc_20051208_orientamenti-zingari_ge.html.
27 Liégeois, Jean Pierre: "Governments and Gypsies: From Rejection to Assimilation."
    In: Rao, Aparna: *The Other Nomads. Peripatetic Minorities in Cross-Cultural Perspective.*
    Böhlau Verlag: Köln 1987, pp. 362 f.
28 Some Roma groups can be designated as peripatetic groups, in the sense of an ethnic
    group or because of language, but with regard to their survival strategies. Their mobility
    is connected with their economic activities. Rao, Aparna: *The other Nomads: Peripatetic
    minorities in cross- cultural perspective.* Böhlau Verlag: Köln 1987. In several European

Catholic Church is conscious of the fact that the majority of Sinti and Roma are now settled, the church justifies a special spiritual welfare for Roma, referring to biblical passages with the context of travel. It is also reflected in the term "Gens de voyage" (people on the move) which is used by pastoral workers and during the masses at the pilgrimage in France.

Many Sinti and Roma criticise that the Catholic Church in the official German paper of the Vatican still uses the social and scientifically constructed racist term "Zigeuner"[29], with its negative connotations in regard to Roma and Sinti's past experiences of exclusion and persecution[30]. These stereotypes and attributions legitimated their exclusion from the major population not only in the past[31] but still today. Even if it is indicated in the document that the term refers to different groups, the Church does not encourage changing the term in the official paper[32].

4.2 Spiritual welfare in local communities

Pastors and pastoral workers in local communities act in a more differentiated manner, instead of using stereotypes or racist terms in their relationships with Roma. At the local level, priests often have very good relationships and friendships in Roma communities with an established basis of trust.

countries, it was forbidden for Sinti and Roma to travel and at the same time it was forbidden for them to settle down. Liégeois, Jean Pierre: "Governments and Gypsies: From Rejection to Assimilation." In: Rao, 1987, pp. 357–372.

29 Maciejewski, Franz: „Elemente des Antiziganismus". In: Giere, Jacqueline: *Die gesellschaftliche Konstruktion des Zigeuners: Zur Genese eines Vorurteils*. Campus Verlag: Frankfurt/New York 1996, p. 22. Reemtsma, Katrin: *Zigeuner in der ethnografischen Literatur: Die „Zigeuner" der Ethnografen*. Fritz Bauer Institut: Frankfurt am Main 1996a, pp. 4–15. Willems, Wim/Lucassen, Leo: "The Church of Knowledge: Representation of Gypsies in Encyclopedias." In: Lucassen Leo/Willems Wim/Cottaar Annemarie: *Gypsies and Other Itinerant Groups. A Socio-Historical Approach*. Centre for the History of Migrants: Univ. of Amsterdam 1998, pp. 45–47.

30 Solms, Wilhelm: „Revision meiner Beiträge zum Tagungsthema." In: Engbring-Romang, Udo/Solms, Wilhelm (Eds.): *Die Stellung der Kirchen zu den deutschen Sinti und Roma*. I-Verb.de: Marburg 2008, pp. 24, 25.

31 Heuß, Herbert: „Die Migration von Roma aus Osteuropa im 19. und 20. Jahrhundert. Historische Anlässe und staatliche Reaktion – Überlegungen zum Funktionswechsel des Zigeuner-Ressentiments." In: Giere, Jacqueline: *Die gesellschaftliche Konstruktion des Zigeuners: Zur Genese eines Vorurteils*. Campus Verlag: Frankfurt/New York 1996, pp. 109 f.

32 Retrieved 02.06.2017, from: http://www.vatican.va/roman_curia/pontifical_councils/migrants/documents/rc_pc_migrants_doc_20051208_orientamenti-zingari_ge.html.

The Catholic Church engages priests, who accompany Sinti and Roma for a period. Their assignments comprise of different activities of pastoral work, such as material and spiritual support, and cooperation with Roma associations, furthering the exchange between local churches and trans-regional networking. Priests and pastoral workers are also engaged in educational and anti-racism work, and they mediate between Roma and local authorities for the provision of rest areas[33]. In addition, they organise masses for commemorating the victims of National Socialism[34].

By the constant attendance over a long term, Roma, Sinti and priests maintain regular contacts. Priests are working mainly with Roma who live in the surrounding of their parish. They visit them frequently and with some families they maintain friendly relationships. Some Roma also travel together with priests to local pilgrimages. Joint masses and the frequent participation at local and transnational pilgrimages encourage communication and exchange between Roma, Sinti and priests in France and in Austria: "I have some families, they are very good friends, where I can come and say, tonight I sleep by you"[35]. The communities of the Catholic Roma accept this pastoral worker in France. If time allows it, he visits them daily and he organises regular meetings: "They come to me, so every month we have a time for prayers, a time for contemplation, and for reflection"[36]. Sometimes he joins mobile Roma communities to travel together to the pilgrimages. At the pilgrimage in Saintes Maries de la Mer, he also met with Roma from Northern France who settled with about ten caravans at the

---

33 From own Interviews.
34 In this way, the Catholic Church contributes to a process of coming to terms with the past. In times of National Socialism, the Church doors have been closed for Roma and Sinti. Moreover, the collaboration between the Church and National Socialists by the opening of Church books contributed to the mass deportation of Roma and Sinti to concentration camps. For a long time, there was no admission of guilt on the part of the Church for the genocide of Roma and Sinti. That is why many Roma turned away from the Catholic Church. There is still a certain suspicion of the institution of the Catholic Church among Roma communities. Through these commemoration ceremonies, the Church tries to improve the relations with Roma and Sinti. Rose, Romani: ...*wenn unsere katholische Kirche uns nicht in ihren Schutz nimmt: Die katholischen Bischöfe und die Deportation der Sinti und Roma nach Auschwitz-Birkenau.* Dokumentations- und Kulturzentrum deutscher Sinti und Roma 2008. Retrieved 14.05.2012, from: http://www.sintiundroma.de/content/downloads/publikationen/online/rose_kath_kirche.pdf.
35 From own Interviews, translated into English by the author.
36 Idem.

outskirts of Saintes Maries de la Mer during the days of pilgrimage. Twenty years ago was the first time that the priest of Saintes Maries de la Mer had encountered Roma in a small chapel in Salon-de-Provence. They asked for participating in the prayer. In 1998, he became a priest of Saintes Maries de la Mer and in addition the responsible pastor for Roma and travellers.

Personal relationships are also important within the pastoral work in Austria: "… they say, come to visit us, we haven´t met for a long time"[37]. It is often the small things that take on importance in these encounters. Recognition and respect is the most important thing for Roma and Sinti. Through the possibility that Roma and Sinti are taking place within this religious space and that they are involved in the decision-making process, the Catholic Church communicates this recognition. Essential is the acceptance of their faith, which sometimes has nothing to do with churchgoing, but more important is the appreciation of their own, very personal spirituality. Each of my interview partners live their faith in their own distinct way. Sometimes it passes from parents to children, sometimes a crisis in life strengthened their faith: "They live with us. Our parents, when we were born, it flowed automatically in, the knowledge of the relation between humans and God and Maria, godmother"[38].

Conclusion

In summary, my chapter gives an insight into the relations between local and transnational spaces. The examples of the pilgrimage in Saintes Maries de la Mer as a transnational event and the more local pilgrimage in Mariazell reflect the diversity of interconnections at different levels: The Catholic Church creates a global community, and the participation in international pilgrimages determines the belonging to a religious space which transcends national borders. Therefore, the participating Roma and Sinti are transnational actors who maintain different relations across nation states. As the study shows, transnational religious networks result from everyday life religiosity and also from transnational networking by religious institutions. These practices can take different forms and are linked to multiple identity constructions.

Roma and Sinti are considered as the largest minority group in Europe. This includes different groups with linguistic and cultural diversity. In almost all areas of life they are confronted with prejudice and marginalisation. The formation of nation states in Europe in the last two hundred years tended to be legitimised

---

37 Idem.
38 Idem.

through an ethnic majority, related to concepts of "culture" on an ideological basis[39]. Through joint pilgrimages, the Catholic Church seeks a dialogue between Roma, Sinti and the majority population, furthering a greater involvement and participation within the Church. On the other hand, at the institutional level, the Church tends to reproduce stereotypes and homogeneous concepts of identity, which legitimated their marginalisation and exclusion for centuries.

Bibliography

Acton, Thomas/Nicolae, Gheorghe: "Citizens of the World and Nowhere: Minority, Ethnic and Human Rights for Roma During the Last Hurrah of the Nation-State." In: Guy, Will (Ed.): *Between Past and Future: The Roma of Central and Eastern Europe*. Univ. of Hertfordshire Press: Hatfield 2001, 54 f.

Appadurai, Arjun: *Modernity at Large: Cultural Dimensions of Globalization*. Univ. of Minnesota Press: Minneapolis/London 1996/2010.

Barany, Zoltan: *The East European Gypsies: Regime, Change, Marginality, and Ethnopolitics*. Cambridge Univ. Press: Cambridge 2002.

Beer, Bettina (Ed.): *Methoden und Techniken der Feldforschung*. Dietrich Reimer Verlag: Berlin 2003.

Cantón Delgado, Manuela: *Croyances protestantes: Stratégies Gitanes*. Religions revisitées Revue trimestrielle numéro 20, 2004, pp. 88–106.

Casanova, José: "Globalizing Catholicism and the Return to a Universal Church." In: Hoeber Rudolph, Susanne/Piscatori, James (Eds.): *Transnational Religion and Fading States*. Westview Press: Colorado/Oxford 1997, pp. 121–143.

Coleman, Simon: *The Globalisation of Charismatic Christianity. Spreading the Gospel of Prosperity*. Cambridge Univ. Press: Cambridge 2000.

Coleman, Simon/Collins, Peter: *Religion, Identity and Change. Perspectives on Global Transformations*. MPG Books: Cornwall 2004.

Engbring-Romang, Udo/Solms, Wilhelm (Eds.): *Die Stellung der Kirchen zu den deutschen Sinti und Roma*. I-Verb.de: Marburg 2008.

Flick, Uwe: *Qualitative Sozialforschung: Eine Einführung*. Rowohlt Taschenbuch Verlag: Hamburg 2002.

Flick, Uwe/Von Kardoff, Ernst/Steinke, Ines (Eds.): *Qualitative Forschung. Ein Handbuch*. Rowohlt Taschenbuch Verlag: Reinbek bei Hamburg 2000/2007.

---

39 Acton, Thomas/Nicolae, Gheorghe: "Citizens of the world and nowhere: Minority, ethnic and human rights for Roma during the last hurrah of the nation-state." In: Guy, Will: *Between Past and Future: The Roma of Central and Eastern Europe*. Univ. of Hertfordshire Press: Hatfield 2001:54 f.

Gay y Blasco, Paloma: Gitano Evangelism: The Emergence of a Politico-Religious Diaspora. Paper presented at the 6th EASA Conference, Krakow 26–29 July 2000. Retrieved 14.5.2012, from: https://transcomm.ox.ac.uk/working%20 papers/WPTC-0104%20Gayyblasco.pdf.

Giere, Jacqueline: *Die gesellschaftliche Konstruktion des Zigeuners: Zur Genese eines Vorurteils.* Campus Verlag: Frankfurt/New York 1996.

Glaser, Barney G./Strauss, Anselm L.: *The Discovery of Grounded Theory: Strategies for Qualitative Research.* Aldine Transaction Publishers: New Brunswick/ London 1967/2009.

Greverus, Ina Maria: *Zigeuner und wir.* Institut für Kulturanthropologie und Europäische Ethnologie der Johann Wolfgang Goethe-Universität: Frankfurt 1975.

Guy, Will: *Between Past and Future: The Roma of Central and Eastern Europe.* Univ. of Hertfordshire Press: Hatfield 2001: 54 f.

Heinschink, Mozes F./Hemetek, Ursula (Eds.): *Roma: Das unbekannte Volk. Schicksal und Kultur.* Böhlau Verlag: Wien/Köln/Weimar 1994.

Hervieu-Léger, Danièle: "Faces of Catholic Transnationalism. In and Beyond France." In: Hoeber Rudolph, Susanne/Piscatori, James (Eds.): *Transnational Religion and Fading States.* Westview Press: Colorado/Oxford 1997.

Heuß, Herbert: „Die Migration von Roma aus Osteuropa im 19. und 20. Jahrhundert. Historische Anlässe und staatliche Reaktion – Überlegungen zum Funktionswechsel des Zigeuner-Ressentiments." In: Giere, Jacqueline (Ed.): *Die gesellschaftliche Konstruktion des Zigeuners: Zur Genese eines Vorurteils.* Campus Verlag: Frankfurt/New York 1996, pp. 109–131.

Hoeber Rudolph, Susanne/Piscatori, James (Eds.): *Transnational Religion and Fading States.* Westview Press: Colorado/Oxford 1997.

Jansen, Dorothea: *Einführung in die Netzwerkanalyse.* Leske und Buderich: Opladen 2003.

Kücher, Gertraud: *Fahrende Roma und Sinti in Österreich im beginnenden 21. Jahrhundert. Eine Untersuchung sozialanthropologischer Theorieansätze ausgehend vom Rastplatz für fahrende Roma und Sinti in Braunau am Inn* (Diplomarbeit). Universität Wien: Wien 2006.

Kurtz, Lester R.: *Gods in the Global Village.* Pine Forge Press: Thousand Oaks 1995.

Levitt, Peggy: *Between God, Ethnicity, and Country: An Approach to the Study of Transnational Religion.* Paper presented at workshop on "Transnational Migration: Comparative Perspectives," June 30–July 1, Princeton University 2001. Retrieved 14.05.2012, from: http://www.transcomm.ox.ac.uk/working% 20papers/Levitt.pdf.

48 Daniela Gruber

Liégeois, Jean Pierre: "Governments and Gypsies: From Rejection to Assimilation." In: Rao, Aparna (Ed.): *The Other Nomads. Peripatetic Minorities in Cross-Cultural Perspective.* Böhlau Verlag: Köln 1987, pp. 357–372.

Liégeois, Jean Pierre: *Roma in Europe.* Council of Europe: Strasbourg 2007.

Lucassen, Leo/Willems, Wim/Cottaar, Annemarie: *Gypsies and Other Itinerant Groups. A Socio-Historical Approach.* Centre for the History of Migrants: Univ. of Amsterdam: Amsterdam 1998.

Maciejewski, Franz: „Elemente des Antiziganismus." In: Gière, Jacqueline (Ed.): *Die gesellschaftliche Konstruktion des Zigeuners: Zur Genese eines Vorurteils.* Campus Verlag: Frankfurt/New York 1996, pp. 9–28.

Mayer, Daniela: "Holy Mother Mary, Pray for Us Sinners – Catholic Pilgrimage in Austria." In: Shahshahani, Soheila (Ed.): *Cities of Pilgrimage.* Lit: Berlin 2009, pp. 127–148.

Mitchell, J.C. (Ed.): *Social Networks in Urban Situations.* University Press: Manchester 1969.

Rao, Aparna: *The Other Nomads: Peripatetic Minorities in Cross-Cultural Perspective.* Böhlau Verlag: Köln 1987.

Reemtsma, Katrin: *Zigeuner in der ethnografischen Literatur: Die „Zigeuner" der Ethnografen.* Fritz Bauer Institut: Frankfurt am Main 1996a.

Reemtsma, Katrin: *Sinti und Roma. Geschichte, Kultur, Gegenwart.* Verlag C.H.Beck: München 1996b.

Rose, Romani: …wenn unsere katholische Kirche uns nicht in ihren Schutz nimmt: Die katholischen Bischöfe und die Deportation der Sinti und Roma nach Auschwitz-Birkenau. Dokumentations- und Kulturzentrum deutscher Sinti und Roma 2008. Retrieved 14.5.2012, from: http:/www.sintiundroma.de/content/downloads/publikationen/online/rose_kath_kirche.pdf.

Schenk, Michael: Soziale Netzwerke und Kommunikation. (Habilitationsschrift der Wirtschafts- und Sozialwissenschaftlichen Fakultät der Universität Augsburg). Mohr: Tübingen 1984.

Schlehe, Judith: „Formen qualitativer ethnografischer Interviews." In: Beer, Bettina (Ed.): *Methoden und Techniken der Feldforschung.* Dietrich Reimer Verlag: Berlin 2003, pp. 71–93.

Schmidt, Christiane: „Analyse von Leitfadeninterviews." In: Flick, Uwe/Von Kardoff, Ernst/Steinke, Ines (Eds.): *Qualitative Forschung. Ein Handbuch.* Rowohlt Taschenbuch Verlag: Reinbek bei Hamburg 2000/2007, pp. 447–455.

Schnegg, Michael/Lang, Hartmut (Eds.): „Netzwerkanalyse. Eine praxisorientierte Einführung." *Methoden der Ehnographie* Heft 1 2002. Retrieved 12.11.2018, from: https://www.researchgate.net/publication/275041134_Die_Netzwerkanalyse_Eine_praxisorientierte_Einfuhrung.

Shahshahani, Soheila (Ed.): *Cities of Pilgrimage*. Lit: Berlin 2009.

Six-Hohenbalken, Maria Anna/Tosic, Jelena (Eds.): *Anthropologie der Migration: Theoretische Grundlagen und interdisziplinäre Aspekte*. Fakultas: Wien 2009.

Six Hohenbalken, Maria Anna: „Religionen in Bewegung." In: Six-Hohenbalken, Maria Anna/Tosic, Jelena (Eds.): *Anthropologie der Migration: Theoretische Grundlagenund interdisziplinäre Aspekte*. Fakultas: Wien 2009, pp. 247–263.

Smith, Michael Peter/Guarnizo, Luis (Eds.): *Transnationalism from Below: Comparative Urban and Community Research*. Volume 6. Transaction Publishers: New Brunswick/London 1998.

Solms, Wilhelm: „Revision meiner Beiträge zum Tagungsthema." In: Engbring-Romang, Udo/Solms, Wilhelm (Eds.): *Die Stellung der Kirchen zu den deutschen Sinti und Roma*. I-Verb.de: Marburg 2008, pp. 20–26.

Strauss, Anselm L.: *Grundlagen qualitativer Sozialforschung: Datenanalyse und Theoriebildung in der empirischen soziologischen Forschung*. Fink: München 1991.

Van der Veer, Peter: *Nation and Religion: Perspectives on Europe and Asia*. Princeton Univ. Press: Princeton, N.Y. 1999.

Van der Veer, Peter: *Transnational religion*. Paper given to the conference on Transnational Migration: Comparative Perspectives. Princeton University, 30 June-1 July 2001. Retrieved 14.5.2012, from: http://www.transcom.ox.ac.uk/working%20papers/WPTC0118%20Van%der%20Veer.pdf.

Vertovec, Steven: *Religion and diaspora*. Paper presented at the conference on New Landscapes of Religion in the West, School of Geography and the Environment, University of Oxford, 27–29 September 2000. Retrieved 14.5.2012, from: http://www.transcomm.ox.ac.uk/working%20papers/Vertovec01.PDF.

Vertovec, Steven: *Transnationalism*. Routledge: New York 2010.

Vossen, Rüdiger: *Roma, Sinti, Gitanos, Gypsies: Zwischen Verfolgung und Romantisierung*. Katalog zur Ausstellung des Hamburgischen Museums für Völkerkunde: Frankfurt a. M./Berlin/Wien 1983.

Willems, Wim/Lucassen, Leo: "The Church of Knowledge: Representation of Gypsies in Encyclopedias." In: Lucassen, Leo/Willems, Wim/Cottaar, Annemarie (Eds.): *Gypsies and Other Itinerant Groups. A Socio-Historical Approach*. Centre for the History of Migrants: Univ. of Amsterdam: Amsterdam 1998.

II Identity

Roberta Rosa and Federica Pastore

Introduction

The notion of identity does not refer to a set of precise elements, since an infinite amount of characteristics contribute to define any individual. Joseph (2006), to give an example, argues that our identity is built by many elements, such as gender, ethnicity, nationality, cultural heritage, age, occupation and social status, but this list could be modified and lengthened further and further. What is certain, is that individual identity is shaped in relation to other people or to other groups of people who act around the individual and thus determine, build or destroy in part the perception that the individual has of himself. As Fabietti claims (1995, p. 43): "To be able to think of myself I must put myself in opposition to someone else"; in other words, my individual identity is the result of the intertwining of multiple collective identities (Todorov, 2010). It is interesting that, as Bauman (2003, p. 15) claims: "Until a few decades ago the identity was not even remotely at the center of our thoughts, it was nothing but an object of philosophical meditation".

To better understand why today's identity is in fact a complex issue, it is necessary to outline the change that this concept has undergone over time, in relation to historical and social changes. If on the one hand, it is true that, as Bauman (2003) supports, the idea of self-determination of one's own life and identity is present since the time of the Enlightenment, when Kant and other illustrious thinkers trusted the faculty of reason as a powerful tool that allows men to compare and choose between the options facing them, on the other hand it is also true that, as Hall (1996) says, in the period of Enlightenment the individual was totally "centred", because his identity was unique and equal from birth to death. The identity of the pre-modern subject was "inherited" unlike the individual of modern society, whose status as bourgeois, for example, was acquired and had therefore to be renewed and maintained in the course of his existence. Despite the overcoming of hereditary privileges and the ability to change their place in society thanks to their own personal abilities, the identity of the individual tended to remain unchanged for the course of his whole life. The stability of identity in the modern age was also determined by cultural factors, such as the strong character of national identity. Although, as Hall (1996) claims, the latter was not imprinted in the genes, people tended to retain it as an integral part of their natural essence, as their own cultural identity (p. 611). The State-Nation of the nineteenth century was based on the myth of the cultural unity of the State, constituted by a homogeneous culture, in which the citizens shared a same language, same traditions and same values. But this idea of unity and absolute homogeneity was in fact only a myth, whose effects remain still today, giving rise to forms of cultural racism. According to Fabietti (1995), people tend to consider cultures as "closed containers in which the authentic traditions of a community, of a people, of an ethnicity or of a nation are placed", thus denying the obvious fact that "all cultures are the product of interactions, exchanges, influences from elsewhere, and no one culture was born 'pure' ".

Today, in discussing problems such as immigration and cultural integration, mass media tend to present the concept of identity, and specifically cultural identity, as a container of well-defined and localised elements, simplifying the multiplicity of each individual by selecting and fixing only a few salient traits that lead to the creation of stereotypes and contribute to widening the distances between "us" and "others". There is no doubt that keeping on building real or conceptual walls is useless and senseless in particular within the European Union.

As Pastore stresses the EU has always been a multicultural society since its inception, a set of nations that have decided to join in respect of each other's diversity, according to the motto: "Unity in diversity". This cultural mosaic has been further enriched in the years thanks to the arrivals of different populations coming today in particular from the African continent. Being multicultural means also being multilingual, and language is one of the many elements that build up our identity and our sense of belonging. Despite the growing interest and promotion of linguistic diversity and human rights by various European institutions (UNESCO, Council of Europe), the influence of monolingual ideology remains in many European States, especially in the field of linguistic rights. In particular, Pastore focuses on the difference between Regional Minorities Linguistic rights and Immigrant Languages rights, focusing on the importance of promoting the latter, which are still not enough protected, being considered languages in but not of Europe.

Concepts like Cross-Border Cooperation (CBC), as discussed by Roberta Rosa, may serve as models for solving identity conflicts by granting additional rights to minorities. After the world wars and due to shifts of borders, the EU and other international organisations faced the problem of new minorities who suddenly found themselves living next to their homeland and who then struggled to uphold their original culture while integrating in their new home country. These identity conflicts might be attenuated by establishing CBC institutions. The theoretical and empirical analysis of examples of Euroregions and European Groupings of Territorial Cooperation (EGTCs) shows to what extent transnational legal cooperation can prove beneficial for minorities by consciously taking linguistic, religious and other cultural differences into account and thus fostering complex forms of identity.

References

Van der Veer, Peter: *Nation and Religion: Perspectives on Europe and Asia.* Princeton Univ. Press: Princeton, N. Y. 1999.

Bauman, Zygmunt: *Educational challenges of the liquid-modern era.* In Diogenes (50) 2003 pp. 15–26.

Fabietti, Ugo: *L'identitá etnica. Storia e critica di un concetto equivoco.* La Nuova Italia Scientifica: Firenze 1995.

Hall, Stuart: 'Who needs "identity"?' In: Hall, Stuart/du Gay, Paul (eds.): *Questions of Cultural Identity.* Sage: London 1996.

Joseph, John. E.: Linguistic identities: Double-edged swords. *Language Problems & Language Planning,* 2006 30(3), pp. 261–267.

Todorov, Tzvetan: *The Fear of Barbarians: beyond the clash of civilization.* The University of Chicago Press: Chicago 2010.

Roberta Rosa

National minorities and cross-border cooperation: solving identity conflicts through integration

Abstract: Cross-border cooperation (CBC), in areas marked by the presence of national minorities, has always represented a controversial issue. Nowadays, several instruments for CBC are available; two of the most institutionalised and popular are Euroregions and European Groupings of Territorial Cooperation (EGTCs), object of this research. This work aims at detecting the nature of CBC in ethnically sensitive areas, to evaluate whether and how it has an impact on the minority population and to estimate whether minorities might be seen as actors of EU integration. Three case studies are analysed through a comparative approach: European Region Tyrol – South Tyrol – Trentino (Italy – Austria), EGTC Pons Danubii (Hungary – Slovakia) and Region Sønderjylland–Schleswig (Denmark – Germany). After an overview on the history and an analysis of the projects organised, attention is devoted to the impact of initiatives on the population by considering their involvement and the fields of intervention. The initial hypothesis is that, despite not being directly designed for minority protection, both Euroregions and EGTCs positively impact minorities, even though to different extents. In particular, the first, being less institutionalised, seem to encourage a broader participation of minority members. Conversely, the second appear to be less involving, since more institutionally framed. As for minorities as bridges for integration, reasons to believe this seem to exist and leave room for further research on the topic.

1 Introduction

Cross-border cooperation (CBC) enacted in areas characterised by ethnic sensitivity, namely marked by the presence of numerically consistent national minorities, has always represented a controversial issue and has been only partially explored, so far.

Over the last fifty years, CBC went through a process of transformation, both in legal and political terms, and evolved from a strategically embedded concept to a more pragmatic and target-oriented one[1]. This has been possible thanks to the development of an *ad hoc* set of legal instruments which encompasses norms

---

1   CBC between divided but ethnically homogeneous areas might be seen as a destabilising factor and interpreted as an attempt to create ethnocentric areas. Over time however, with the process of Europeanisation, cooperation became a functional means to achieve common goals.

from a complex multi-level reality (e.g. Council of Europe, European Union and domestic legislation). Several instruments for CBC came into existence, among these there are the popular Euroregions and European Groupings of Territorial Cooperation (EGTCs), units of analysis of the research.

This work aims at detecting the theoretical and empirical nature of CBC in areas inhabited by national minorities, to evaluate through the lenses of a top-down approach whether and how they have an impact on the minority population and, secondly, to estimate whether minorities might be seen as key for European integration.

Moving from these two research questions, a comparative method has been chosen to delve into the relation between CBC and national minorities and applies to three case studies: Euregio Tyrol-South Tyrol-Trentino (Italy and Austria), EGTC Pons Danubii (Hungary and Slovakia) and Region Sønderjylland–Schleswig (Denmark and Germany).

After a brief overview on the history of the regions concerned, the work focuses on the form and the scope of cooperation of each of the above-mentioned EGTCs and Euroregion. In particular, the initiatives organised are focused on, to evaluate their impact on the population by considering the involvement of minority members, their effectiveness in stimulating a dialogue between different cultures, and the fields of intervention targeted.

Overall, the three cases analysed suggest that CBC may be a useful instrument to handle national diversity and regional homogeneity and to allow national, minority and cross-border identities to coexist. Historically contested areas have managed to find their place in the European space and to constitute new fora for integration between different cultures and people whose identity is distinctively shaped by constant interaction.

2 Cross-border cooperation: evolution of the concept

Before analysing concrete case studies, some remarks on the concept of cross-border cooperation (CBC)[2] shall be provided. CBC is not new in international relations; in fact, the first initiatives to establish permanent contact across

---

2   Also referred to as trans-frontier cooperation, defined by the Council of Europe as "any concerted action designed to reinforce and foster neighbourly relations between territorial communities or authorities" in the European Outline Convention on Transfrontier Co-operation between Territorial Communities or Authorities, Madrid, 21 May 1980 CETS No. 106, retrieved 01.03.2018, from http://www.coe.int/en/web/conventions/full-list/-/conventions/treaty/.

national borders date back to the 1950s, but it was only after the end of the Cold War that CBC started being devoted attention to[3]. The development of coopera-tion on a cross-border dimension encountered many obstacles, since it required a major change in the meaning of borders. Until the end of World War II, a con-ception of borders as barriers had prevailed but a process of de-bordering grad-ually started in the 1950s, when the first European Communities were created, and since then, borders changed their nature to filters and eventually to zones of contact[4].

Openness and permeability of borders are assumed as important preconditions to CBC but they are not sufficient when this is enacted in border areas inhabited by national minorities. In fact, cooperation between ethnically homogeneous border areas might be considered as a destabilising factor and a possible attempt to establish ethnocentric areas with a strong cultural identity[5] that strongly opposes that of the home state. Therefore, according to Engl and Woelk (2007) several additional factors deserve consideration that influence the participation of minorities in CBC. These are (1) the presence of a kin-state at the border, (2) the quality of the majority-minority relations, (3) the degree of institutionalisation and (4) the political and strategic orientation of the relevant state. If the goals of cooperation are perceived merely functional and oriented towards the improvement of the well-being of the population, there would be no institutional or political obstacles to their development; on the contrary, if a state perceives that allowing CBC would represent a threat to its unity and integrity also in terms of national identity, it would not allow any form of cooperation[6].

---

3 After the end of the Cold War a new commitment to peace and integration developed. In addition, since border territories suffered from the same problems caused by the war and linked to their peripheral position, a news idea emerged that cooperation could bring considerable advantages to territories. Palermo, Francesco: "The New Nomos of Cross-border Cooperation". In: Palermo, Francesco/Poggeschi, Giovanni/ Rautz, Günther/Woelk, Jens (eds.): Globalization, Technologies and Legal Revolution. Nomos: Baden-Baden, 2012, p. 75.

4 Ferrara, Walter/Pasi Paolo: "Introduzione: regioni transfrontaliere, cooperazione transfrontaliera ed euroregioni". In: Pasi Paolo/Ferrara Walter (eds.): *Come Funzionano le Euroregioni, Esplorazione in Sette Casi*, Istituto di Sociologia Internazionale di Gorizia: Gorizia, 2000, pp. 1–12.

5 Just, Roger: "Triumph of the Ethos". In Tonkin, Elizabeth/McDonald, Maryon/ Chapman, Malcolm K. (eds.): History and Ethnicity. Routledge: London, 1989, p. 77, p. 86.

6 Engl, Alice/Woelk, Jens: "Cross-border Cooperation and Minorities in Eastern Europe: Still Waiting for a Chance? A Summary and Evaluation of the Four Case

As the link between CBC and minorities was highly both politically and ideologically charged until the end of the Cold War, it was often seen with suspicion mainly by the majority population and by the authorities of the home states. However, as over the 1990s the process of EU integration deepened, EU internal borders started to gradually lose importance, and supra-national actors (EU, Council of Europe, OSCE) addressed the matter of CBC considering its potential link with minority issues for the first time very promptly. Eventually minorities were entitled to a "right to CBC", as stated in several international treaties and national norms[7].

With the development and evolution of a specific legal set framing the link between CBC and minorities both at international and national level, the acquisition of a functional and target-oriented approach was realised, and this led to the reduction of ideological commitment. On these bases, a wide set of legal instruments for CBC came into existence, ranging from the less institutionalised Euroregions, provided by international law,[8] to the highly framed EU instrument, the European Groupings of Territorial Cooperation (EGTCs)[9].

The main difference between Euroregions and EGTCs lies in the attribution of legal personality, enjoyed by the latter and not by the first[10]. This aspect confers

---

Studies". In: Bloed, Arie et al., *European Yearbook of Minority Issues*, Brill: Leiden, 2007, pp. 235 – 247.

7   See Art.17 of the Framework Convention on the Protection of National Minorities, Art. 3 of the Madrid Outline Convention and Art. 10 of the European Charter of Local Self-government (CoE), Art. 16 of the Bolzano/Bozen Recommendations, Paragraph 32 of the Document of the Copenhagen Meeting of the Conference on the Human Dimension (OSCE) as well as *ad hoc* norms of domestic legislation.

8   Structures whose ultimate goal lies in the "promotion of cross-border cooperation between border regions, local entities, regional authorities, social partners and all other actors on matters such as culture, education, tourism, economic issues and any other aspect of daily life", as stated in the European Parliament Resolution on the Role of "Euroregions" in the Development of Regional Policy, P6_TA(2005)0448, retrieved 01.03.2018 from http://www.europarl.europa.eu/sides/getDoc.dotype=TA&language =EN&reference=P6-TA- 2005-0448.

9   Defined as "cooperation instrument at Community level […] invested with legal personality". Regulation (EC) No. 1082/2006 of the European Parliament and of the Council of 5 July 2006 on a European Grouping of Territorial Cooperation (EGTC), amended by Regulation (EU) 13 February 2013 of the European Parliament and of the Council of 17 December 2013.

10   The attribution of legal personality enables EGTCs to: have their own budget, employ staff affiliated to specific organs, hold property, participate in legal proceedings. Euroregions, on the contrary, do not dispose of such opportunities. Spinaci, Gianluca/Vara-Arribas, Gracia: "The European Grouping of Territorial Cooperation

greater independence, for example, from the central government but at the same time it can translate into demanding bureaucratic processes and overall complexity, therefore it requires adequate capacity and facilities. On the other hand, Euroregions are ruled under private law, since they are not "legal persons", and their structure is less rigid, compared to the highly legally framed EGTCs. To understand more specifically the role of CBC structures, the following comparative analysis of concrete case studies may be useful.

3 Comparative analysis: main findings

As mentioned, three border areas have been selected: Italy–Austria, Slovakia–Hungary and Denmark–Germany. In these territories, two European Groupings of Territorial Cooperation (EGTCs) and one Euroregion can be found, respectively: EGTC European Region Tyrol – South Tyrol – Trentino, Pons Danubii EGTC and the Region Sønderjylland–Schleswig. In all these three contexts, the borders had shifted several times as a consequence of World War I and II and thus many people found themselves to become members of a national minority on a territory (home-state), bordering their kin-state, in which the dominant culture was different from their one thus having strong repercussions on their individual and group identity. By reason of this, even though CBC has been thought as a means of integration which implies the preservation of cultural diversity, it has also been used to preserve cultural homogeneity.

These three cases selected are particularly interesting to be looked at, considering briefly their historical background, the form and scope of cooperation selected as well as the impact on minorities and their contribution to integration.

3.1 European region Tyrol – South Tyrol – Trentino

In Italy, the German-speaking minority living in South Tyrol, that represents 70 % of its population, had to struggle to gain minority rights since the aftermath of World War I, when Trentino and South Tyrol were awarded to Italy, often with the intervention of their kin-state Austria. Nowadays this minority is enumerated among the best protected ones, due to the autonomous territorial arrangements put in place in their territory[11].

(EGTC): New Spaces and Contracts for European Integration?" EIPASCOPE (2), European Institute of Public Administration, 2009, p. 9.

11 Palermo, Francesco/Woelk, Jens: "Diritto costituzionale comparato dei gruppi e delle minoranze", Cedam: Padova, 2008, p. 242.

The process to set up an EGTC including Tyrol, South Tyrol and Trentino was demanding and debated between the national and the local governments, due to the initial reluctant attitude of the Italian government. Since its birth in 2011, the projects of this European Region have been targeted on the environmental and cultural/linguistic characteristic of the territory. As it can be read in the Statute of the EGTC[12], the fields of intervention are education, culture, energy, sustainable development, health, research and innovation, economy and mountain farming and environment. The activities carried out translate into practice, *inter alia*, in the organisation of exhibitions, institution of awards for students and scholarships and the development of many joint research and learning programs concerning, for example, environmental and minority issues. In the several projects and studies carried out, the awareness of living in a territory characterised by a plurality of ethnicities and languages has often been the starting point, and it has been identified as the key for integration of different cultural groups. An interesting point to raise is also the practical implication of the activities of this EGTC: New trains and cycle paths, for example, have been put in place to improve mobility within the three territories. From the overview on the projects implemented, a centralised approach can be detected. All activities are promoted by the organs of the EGTC and open to the population for participation. Even though the EGTC European Region Tyrol – South Tyrol – Trentino started as a spontaneous cooperation agreement through a bottom-up process, once it has been created, there remained less room for spontaneity.

3.2 Pons Danubii EGTC

Slovakia, as happened to its neighbouring countries, became home to a sizeable Hungarian minority when Hungary was punished in territorial terms after World War I. Overall, the acquisition of formerly Hungarian territories by other countries resulted in an ethnic patchwork. To face this, Hungary had been playing the role of a strong kin-state, even implementing legislation specifically addressing "Hungarians living abroad" and raising suspicion among other states. A Slovak minority on the Hungarian territory also exists, contributing to create a specular reality[13].

---

12 Statute of the European Grouping of Territorial Cooperation "Euregio Tyrol – South Tyrol – Trentino", 14 June 2011, retrieved 16.08.2017 from:http://www.europaregion.info/downloads/Euregio-EVTZ-Statut-GECTstatuteCastelThun20110614.pdf.
13 European Academy of Bolzano, Best Practices of Minority Protection in Europe, Legal Country Study: Hungary, Bolzano, 2009, p. 4.

The context of this second case is quite different: Less privileged in eco-nomic terms, the border area between Slovakia and Hungary has become home to a great number of EGTCs with more or less functional aims. The Pons Danubii EGTC is situated in the western part of the border area, and since 2010 it seeks to establish cross-border cohesion and implement projects to enhance the quality of life of its citizens. The approach adopted is very target-oriented: three project areas have been identified (labour, media, infrastruc-ture) and actions were planned to produce concrete results: The establishment of a common labour office, of a bilingual TV channel and the construction of a cycle path are the main achievements of the strategic planning of the last years that shall promote the mutual knowledge and ease collaboration between minorities and majorities. In fact, in this area, proud and consciousness of being "Hungarian" or "Slovak" still play a great role in the definition of almost separate groups that still look at historical circumstances with resentment[14], therefore cooperation is of major importance. In particular, the development of the bilingual TV channel broadcasting documentaries, programs for chil-dren, etc. is an important achievement since by implementing bilingualism and favouring a better reciprocal understanding, discrimination is prevented and social cohesion strongly promoted. Gathering the two cultural groups in contact makes it possible to go beyond cultural belonging; it can stimulate the awareness of living in a multicultural territory and of its benefits. The promo-tion of language can lead also to a better integration in other fields of society, such as the labour market.

As in the previous case, activities of the EGTC are planned by its personnel and do not leave much room for direct involvement of citizens, who are often mere recipients of the outcome of the projects. What renders this case study interesting is its geographical position and the economic disadvantage. Being in a lugging-behind region, any additional means to improve the situation is welcome by both the local population and the local government. In this sense, gaining advantage from projects commonly managed by bordering local com-munities could encourage mutual engagement and bring benefits both to the territory and to people, aspects that on the long term could translate into more European integration and into development of a blurring border identity.

---

14 Palermo, Francesco "Transfrontier Co-operation as a Means to maintain Ethnocultural Diversity: Limits and Opportunities", in: Gémesi, Ferenc, *Minorities in a Seamless Europe. The Role of Transfrontier Cooperation in Maintaining Ethno-cultural Diversity*, Office of the Prime Minister of the Republic of Hungary, 2010.

3.3 Region Sønderjylland–Schleswig

Similarly, to the previous case in terms of presence of a kin-state and shifts of borders accompanied by political controversies, the Danish-German case is also interesting for its presence of a German minority in Syddanmark and a Danish minority in Schleswig-Holstein which cooperate in the frame of a Euroregion, the Region Sønderjylland–Schleswig.

This third case is qualitatively different from the other two considered: Whereas the first two units of analysis were EGTCs, here a Euroregion is dealt with. The recent history of the two territories involved has not been as violent and detrimental as that of the other two border regions analysed so far, the premises for cooperation were more encouraging and based on a long experience of intercultural dialogue. In this case, in fact, both Denmark and Germany play the double role of kin-states and home-states and this easy reciprocal understanding, in addition, the recent history of the area has not been violent and detrimental as in the other cases considered. The Euroregion was created in 1997 to face problems stemming from the peripheral position of the area and forces were combined to face challenges in the fields of economic development, job market, culture, education, health and environment[15]. The main goal was (and still remains) improving the economic potential of the area and the general living conditions of the two communities, German and Danish, with a focus on the promotion of mutual knowledge of the two languages. The pursuit of these aims is realised through several activities, for example, to give equal status to both languages and favour cultural exchange, annual meetings are organised and a language project created to promote the neighbour's culture and teach children basic words. In particular, the projects included in the strategy *Kurskultur* aim at promoting a cultural exchange, e.g. of students and teachers. For example, teacher may access a website where they can get in touch, discuss and download bilingual learning contents. This attention to language is relevant because when people have learnt how to communicate, they can better cooperate in everyday life aspects. In addition, meetings of minority artists are held at a *Multikulturhaus* to promote both artistic production as well as a (euro)regional culture encompassing elements from the Danish and German identity. As concerns the labour market, like the Pons Danubii EGTC, this Euroregion created an infocentre and a regional job agency. Attention is also devoted to newcomers that do not identify themselves

---

15 Malloy, Tove, "Competence Analysis: National Minorities as a Standortfaktor in the German- Danish Border Region" – Working with each other, for each other, EURAC Research: Bolzano, 2007, p. 61.

neither with the German nor with the Danish minorities; they are also involved in the activities and the emergence of a new Euroregional culture and identity which is a mixture of the two prevailing in the region is becoming a reality.

The peculiarity of this case lies in a societal aspect. Both on the Danish and on the German side of the border, there exists a vast plethora of associations and NGOs dealing with different issues that are involved in the implementation of the projects of the Euroregion and function as networks for minority members. This civic activism represents an advantage for the Euroregion since associations of minority members can be very useful to reach the citizens. Conversely, citizens might participate directly in the activities of the Euroregions both as recipient individuals and as members of these associations thus gaining an additional chance for involvement.

3.4 Comparison

Cross-border cooperation in the three cases described has roots in similar geographic circumstances but then developed along different lines according to peculiar political, historical and economic aspects, as explained in the previous paragraphs.

The two EGTCs and the Euroregion all pursue the ultimate goal of increasing territorial cohesion and also of improving the living conditions of their inhabitants, mainly national minorities. This empirical analysis has sought at first to assess whether CBC practices have an impact on minorities and their quality of life, even though not specifically designed for this.

Overall, this question can be answered positively, in fact, the framework and the instruments provided CBC might be interpreted as additional means to preserve and maintain the minority culture, even though always implying an interaction with the majority, since all activities involve both the majority and the minority population. As for the fields of intervention, some differences emerged from the study: A great variety of areas (labour, infrastructure, media, art, schooling) is touched upon, according to the needs of the region and of the population, but culture has always a central role. On these bases, some remarks can be drawn concerning the effective involvement of minorities in the activities of the cross-border entities. Participation in initiatives varies from case to case. In the two EGTCs, people can be considered as pure recipient of the initiatives promoted while there seems to be more room for a broader direct participation in the Region Sønderjylland–Schleswig, where the implementation of the projects is done together with and through associations managed by people for the people. This additional civic level functions as amplifier of the effects looked for by the Euroregion. By engaging in direct relations, citizens may become an active part in the policies of the cross-border structure, and in this way also minority members have the chance to form stable networks in the regional context. In addition, it can be affirmed that minorities could possibly be a key for EU integration. Adopting a bottom-up approach, minorities that had been given the opportunity to cooperate with co-ethnics on a cross-border dimension may become important bridge-builders on the European scene to promote integration from below, an aspect that shall not be underestimated.

4 Conclusion

After this overview, it can be asserted that historically contested areas have managed to find their place in the European arena and happened to constitute new cross-border territorial entities, which developed into minority-friendly contexts. By applying intra-ethnic CBC, "minority status" may potentially loose its negative connotation (usually it refers to a group which is separate from another, a greater one), since initiatives of Euroregions and EGTCs have the potential to create integration and mutual trust. On these grounds, the analysis of the case study has shown that CBC brings concrete benefits to minorities inhabiting border territories even though a clear but multifaceted picture emerged, according to the forms, means and targets adopted.

By taking into consideration border areas as units of analysis, a mention to identity matters cannot be neglected. Minorities and majorities interact daily and, in a long-term perspective, cooperation can lead to increasing integration and development of a new cross-border identity, co-existing with the minority or majority one.

Euroregions and EGTCs can be considered as fora that favour dialogue between different cultures that, in particular, offer the chance to engage in mutual respectful relationships and to eventually recognise diversity as a peculiar and distinctive aspect in everyday life.

Bibliography

Council of Europe, Charter of Local Self-Government, Strasbourg, 15 October 1985, CETS No. 122, retrieved 01.03.2018, from http://www.coe. int/en/web/conventions/full-list/-/conventions/treaty/122.

Council of Europe, European Outline Convention on Transfrontier Co-operation between Territorial Communities or Authorities, Madrid, 21 May 1980 CETS No.106, retrieved 01.03.2018, from http://www.coe.int/en/web/conventions/fulllist/-/conventions/treaty/106.

Council of Europe, Framework Convention for the Protection of National Minorities, 1998, retrieved 01.03.2018, from http://www.conventions.coe.int/Treaty/en/Treaties/Html/157.htm.

EGTC Tyrol – South Tyrol – Trentino, Statute of the European Grouping of Territorial Cooperation, "Euregio Tyrol – South Tyrol – Trentino", 14th June 2011, retrieved 01.03.2018 from: http://www.europaregion.info/downloads/EuregioEVTZStatutGECTstatuteCastelThun20110614.pdf.

Engl, Alice/Woelk, Jens: "Cross border Cooperation and Minorities in Eastern Europe: Still Waiting for a Chance? A Summary and Evaluation of the Four Case Studies". In: Bloed, Arie et al.: *European Yearbook of Minority Issues*, Brill: Leiden, 2007.

European Academy of Bolzano, Best Practices of Minority Protection in Europe, Legal Country Study: Hungary, Bolzano, 2009.

European Parliament and Council, Regulation of 5 July 2006 on a European Grouping of Territorial Cooperation (EGTC), Official Journal of the European Union L 210 of 31.07.2006. Amended by Regulation (EU) 13/02/2013 of the European Parliament and of the Council of 17 December 2013.

European Parliament, Resolution on the Role of "Euroregions" in the Development of Regional Policy, P6_TA (2005) 0448, 1 December 2005, retrieved 16.08.2017 from: http://eurlex.europa.eu/legalcontent/EN/TXT/uri=uriserv:g24007http://www.europarl.europa.eu/sides/getDoc.dotype=TA&language=EN&reference=P6-TA2005-0448.

Ferrara, Walter/Pasi, Paolo: "Introduzione: regioni transfrontaliere, cooperazione transfrontaliera ed euroregioni". In: Pasi, Paolo/Ferrara, Walter (eds.): *Come Funzionano le Euroregioni, Esplorazione in Sette Casi*, Istituto di Sociologia Internazionale di Gorizia: Gorizia, 2000.

Just, Roger: "Triumph of the Ethos". In Tonkin, Elizabeth/McDonald, Maryon/Chapman, Malcolm K. (eds.): *History and Ethnicity*, Routledge: London, 1989.

Malloy, Tove: "Competence Analysis: National Minorities as a Standortfaktor in the German- Danish Border Region – Working with each other, for each other", EURAC Research: Bolzano, 2007.

Organization for Security and Co-operation in Europe, Bolzano/BozenRecommendations on National Minorities in Inter-state Relations & Explanatory Report, 2 October 2008, retrieved 01.08.2017, from http://www.osce.org/hcnm/33633.

Organization for Security and Co-operation in Europe, Document of the Copenhagen Meeting of the Conference on the Human Dimension of the CSCE, 29 June 1990, retrieved 01.03.2018, from http://www.osce.org/it/odihr/elections/14304.

Organization for Security and Co-operation in Europe (OSCE), High Commissioner on National Minorities, Bolzano/Bozen Recommendation on National Minorities in Inter-State Relations & Explanatory Report, The Hague, June 2008, retrieved 01.03.2018, from http://www.osce.org/hcnm/33633.

Palermo, Francesco: "Transfrontier Co-operation as a Means to Maintain Ethnocultural Diversity: Limits and Opportunities". In: Gémesi, Ferenc (ed.): *Minorities in a Seamless Europe. The Role of Transfrontier Cooperation in Maintaining Ethno-cultural Diversity*, Office of the Prime Minister of the Republic of Hungary: Budapest 2010.

Palermo, Francesco: "The New Nomos of Cross-border Cooperation". In: Palermo, Francesco/Poggeschi, Giovanni/Rautz, Günther/Woelk, Jens (eds.): *Globalization, Technologies and Legal Revolution*, Nomos: Baden-Baden, 2012.

Palermo, Francesco/Woelk, Jens: Diritto costituzionale comparato dei gruppi e delle minoranze, Cedam: Padova, 2008.

Spinaci, Gianluca/Vara-Arribas, Gracia: "The European Grouping of Territorial Cooperation (EGTC): New Spaces and Contracts for European Integration?" EIPASCOPE (2), European Institute of Public Administration, 2009. Retrieved 7.10.2018, from https://www.cvce.eu/obj/the_european_grouping_of_territorial_cooperation_egtc_new_spaces_and_contracts_for_european_integration_2009-en-98711a87-5d95-41da-918c-20401d327444.html.

Federica Pastore

The role of language in the integration process

Abstract: Nowadays immigration constitutes one of the greatest challenges for Europe, since it forces us to rethink the way we conduct our lives from a social and a political point of view, casting doubts also on those aspects we consider fixed and settled, as for instance our identity. This situation leads to a collective vulnerability, stirring up fear-driven and xenophobic attitudes, which appear to be paradoxical in our multicultural and intercon- nected world. In this respect language plays a significant role, and the aim of this work is to stress the lack of attention to the promotion and preservation of the immigrant languages (IM). This disregard is linked to the artificial idea of national homogeneity, which paves the way for a will to preserve the supposed purity of our own cultural and linguistic identity, putting aside the importance of preserving and promoting the languages of newcomers. Beyond official languages, only regional minority languages (RM) after 1992 enjoy some recognition thanks to "The European Charter of Regional or Minority Languages" as will be described. The status of the IM is clearly inferior to that of RM, but this seems to be paradoxical since immigrant and regional languages are both minorities present in the European landscape, and what is claimed for RM should be valid also for IM (for instance that the vitality of the whole society is animated by the linguistic and cultural diversity of minority groups). The paper emphasizes how retaining and promoting IM can be a means rather than a barrier for social inclusion in the new society. It is in fact wrongly believed that the language of origin could slower the acquisition of the new language and there- fore the inclusion into the new society. There is no doubt that learning the host country's language is of vital importance, but assuring more dignity and esteem to IM would allow newcomers to feel accepted and free to express their own identity, instead of feeling judged and therefore forced to confine in parallel ghettoised societies.

1 Introduction

Europe is a multicultural society, for years it has been a land of immigration and emigration. But today more than ever it seems to be passing through a time of great change and anxiety, due to migrants' movements, described by newspapers and media as "invasions", casting worries on our sense of security and identity, and therefore making even more difficult the process of integration and accep- tance of other nationalities. Public opinion and politicians underline the eco- nomic and political aspects of immigration, more concerned about raising walls than finding durable solutions for a real, mutual understanding between cultures. In this international context, identity is an extremely important element that needs to be further discussed in the academic and public space, since it is a complex and instable issue. The question of recognition of different cultural identities is here analysed from a linguistic point of view.

A powerful, though often overlooked, means for understanding and getting to know a different culture is in fact language. In this chapter, language is not considered only as means of communication, useful in our everyday life, and therefore the focus is not on the acquisition of the host country's official language. Language has in fact also a symbolic value for its speakers, because, as described in Chapter 2, it is deeply related to identity. Starting from this premise, it is clear that having the possibility to retain your own language is in fact a very important element in the process of integration. Taking into account the multilingual European context, policies should have high regard for all the languages spoken on the European territory, in particular for those of the newcomers, since language is one of the few elements still attached to their origins. However, immigrant languages (IM) do not enjoy the same rights to be protected and preserved as national official languages or regional minority languages (RM). There is a wrong idea that fostering immigrant languages in Europe could be "dangerous" to our European or national identity, therefore they do not deserve rights. Moreover, there is an erroneous belief that the mother tongue of the migrants can only delay the acquisition of the new language of the host country. As described in Chapter 3, the European linguistic policy seems to be contradictory, stating on the one hand that Europe is a multicultural and therefore multilingual society and trying to promote diversity as a European label, yet on the other hand, still not giving to IM the same rights as official languages or at least as RM. As clarified in Section 3.1, there are many biases toward the retention and protection of immigrant languages, which could actually enhance and facilitate integration, rather than slowing down this process.

2 Language and identity

Language is one of the many elements which construct our identity, having not only a practical communicative function but also a symbolic and metaphoric one. As Lo Bianco (2013)[1] declared in an interview: "Languages are both tools and symbols, languages mediate both material and symbolic worlds, what I mean by this is that languages are both very practical, helping or hindering access to jobs and social opportunities and also markers of belonging and

---

1   Lo Bianco, Jo "An interview with Joseph Lo Bianco", from: www.channelviewpublications. wordpress.com/2013/08/06/an-interview-with-joseph-lo-bianco/.

identity". This is why when it comes to talking about integration the relevance of languages cannot be undervalued: "(...) they play an important role since they are markers of belonging, both for the migrants and for the host societies" (Council of Europe 2008, p. 6)[2]. It must be considered that the close connection to identity has constantly related language to social and political issues. It is enough to mention linguistic dynamics during colonisation, when speaking the language of the colonizer meant assuming a culture, a civilisation, the "value" of the European colonizer. A man who has a language consequently possesses the world expressed and implied by that language. Nowadays a greater "value" is given to those newcomers who can speak properly the language of the host country, because this seems to express a real will to integrate in the new society. But promoting and valuing only the host country's language leads to assimilation, rather than real integration. Integration is two-folded and implies also the acceptance and recognition of the newcomers' cultural identities. For the European Union, language diversity constitutes a real contradictory issue: on the one hand diversity, multiculturality and multilingualism are declared and promoted as a fundamental element in today's Europe; on the other hand, a lack of linguistic and cultural rights for the newcomers is also evident. This attitude is encouraged by the presence of an obsolete monolingual paradigm, which has its origin in the nineteenth-century construction of the Nation-State which "(...) enforced the belief that a national language should correspond to each Nation-State, and that this language should be regarded as a core value of national identity" (Extra and Yagmur 2004, p. 14)[3]. This conviction results in what Gogolin (1997)[4] defines the monolingual habitus: "(...) the deep-seated habit of assuming monolingualism as the norm in a nation" (pp. 40,41), which leads to an enhancement of the host country language, more than a promotion and protection of the migrants' language of origin.

---

2   Council of Europe "The role of languages in policies for the integration of adult migrants". Concept paper by Jean-Claude Beacco, 2008, from:www.coe.int/t/dg4/linguistic/Publications_EN.asp.
3   Extra, G., & Yagmur, K.: "Urban multilingualism in Europe immigrant minority languages at home and school". Clevedon, Avon, England: Multilingual Matters, 2004.
4   Gogolin, Ingrid: "The 'monolingual habitus' as the common feature in teaching in the language of the majority in different countries". Per Linguam 13(2), 1997, pp. 40,41.

3 European linguistic policy

According to Eurobarometer statistical study "Europeans and their languages"[5], in Europe there are 23 officially recognised languages, more than 60 regional or minority languages and around 250 extra-European languages, not official, not regional, but still spoken in the European country. This being the case, there is no doubt that Europe is "multilingual", as defined by the Council of Europe:

> Multilingualism refers to the presence in a geographical area, large or small, of more than one 'variety of language' i.e. the mode of speaking of a social group whether it is formally recognised as a language or not (…).

Although the European Union strives to protect its rich linguistic diversity and to promote language learning, it must be stated that actions in favour of the promotion of multilingualism have not led yet to a sufficient level of equality among languages, especially as regards immigrant minority languages (IM).

Those languages are considered "languages *in* but not *of* Europe" as Nic Craith (2006, p. 173)[6] states, and their status is clearly inferior to that of the regional minority languages (RM) which, all in all, starting from the conclusion of the "European Charter of Regional or Minority Languages" ECRLM of 1992[7], enjoy some recognition and protection. In particular, the Charter guarantees to speakers of regional minorities the right to political representation and dialogue with governments and public administrations in their own language, stressing also that the vitality of the whole society is animated by the linguistic and cultural diversity of minority groups, whose traditions must therefore be preserved. In addition, in 1995, in order to ensure one of the fundamental priorities of the Council of Europe, namely the unity between its members and the preservation of their common heritage, it was stipulated the Convention for the Protection of National Minorities (FCPNM), in which the role of traditional languages and cultures also appeared, as guarantor of this priority. Nic Craith (2006) stresses that Article 5 explicitly promotes the development of the culture of national minorities and the protection of the essential elements of their identity, specifically their religion, their language, their traditions and their cultural heritage. The following chapter even encourages intercultural dialogue and respect between individuals living in a particular territory, irrespective of their ethnic,

---

5   Eurobarometer, Report: Europeans and their languages, 2012.
6   Nic Craith Màireàd, "Europe and the Politics of Language Citizens, Migrants and Outsiders", Basingstoke and New York, Palgrave Macmillan Ed., 2006.
7   Council of Europe, "European Charter of Minority Languages", 1992. http://www.coe.int/it/web/conventions/full-list/-/conventions/rms/090000168007c095.

cultural, linguistic or religious identity. Immigrant languages do not enjoy the same privileges in Europe, although they are indeed new languages of the European landscape, belonging to communities of speakers who conceive them not only as a communication tool, but also as a symbol of identity, able to maintain the sense of belonging to their origins. Kloss (1971)[8] specifically outlines four typical arguments behind the denial of rights for the IM and the perceived need to learn the host country language instead:

(a) The tacit compact theory holds that immigrants, by seeking to move to a new country, agree to adapt to the majority language of the new country.
(b) The take-and-give theory states that most immigrants will be better off economically in the new country, and therefore should give themselves over completely to the majority culture of the new country.
(c) The anti-ghettoisation theory contends that immigrants who maintain their previous culture are isolating themselves and their children from the mainstream of national life, while at the same time they are unable to keep up with cultural life of their country of origin.
(d) The national unity theory worries that immigrant groups that maintain their language will become a disruptive force in national politics, and therefore will make the host countries unstable.

All these assumptions reveal an attachment to the nation-state ideology and the monolingual habitus, which refuses to recognize the existence of multiple and transnational identities perceived as elements that undermine social cohesion. As regards specifically the first three points, it is clear that learning the language of the host country is undoubtedly a need to find a job and to enter the new society, avoiding ghettoisation, but what must also be taken into serious consideration is that many people do not choose to leave voluntarily their countries and their traditions. Giving value and social recognition to their language of origin is therefore of vital importance for them (Extra and Yagmur 2004)[9]. Moreover, denying any recognition seems to overlook the fact that those who arrive in Europe can settle there in the long term, and that over time those who should have been "passing by" migrants are becoming second or third generations of European citizens. Therefore, they are entitled as much as the regional minority

---

8   Kloss, Heinz. "Language Rights and Immigrant Groups". International Migration Review 5. 1971, pp. 250–268.
9   Ibid.

groups to be protected in their cultural diversity. As Rubio Marìn (2003, p. 138)[10] stresses, the basic idea behind the gap between RM and IM is that the regional minority groups have been forced to be incorporated in a State and therefore deprived of the right to define themselves as other Nations have done at the time of their births. Those who emigrate from their own country instead, decide to consciously put themselves in the minority position with respect to the rest of the society and therefore become responsible for learning the new language of the host country, putting aside their own. However, as already said, this cannot be stated for everyone.

Among the main reasons why linguistic rights are not granted to immigrants, is also the fear that their mother tongue limits the learning of the majority language and therefore the integration itself. On the contrary, as Kymlicka (2001)[11] suggests, the integration process can be made easier by securing public services and the same education in the mother tongue of the newly arrived migrant in a new country, since the learning of the legal, administrative and cultural system can be facilitated from the use of its own language of origin, rather than inhibited.

3.1 Retaining Immigrant Languages as a means of social inclusion

Disregarding IM languages and fostering only the need to learn the host country language does not lead to a better integration or a quicker acquisition of the new language, but rather to social exclusion and alienation. In this regard, European institutions should actively try to promote the importance of innovating education systems so that support is given to children with a migrant background, first of all by teaching them the language of the host country, but also trying to emphasize the need of valuing and preserving the L1 (first language) of those children. In the education field, Cummins (2011)[12] often stresses a lot the fact that the fostering of multilingualism, and specifically the languages of origin of the newly arrived, is a general tendency to see L1 as an element that could cause a slower acquisition of the new language and lower academic achievement.

---

10 Rubio-Marin R., "Exploring the boundaries of Language Rights: Insiders, Newcomers and Natives", in Nomos: Secession and new determination, Jstor, 2003, pp. 136–173.
11 Kymlicka Will, Politics in the Vernacular: Nationalism, Multiculturalism, and Citizenship, Oxford, Oxford University Press, 2001.
12 Cummins, Jim: "The intersection of cognitive and sociocultural factors in the development of reading comprehension among immigrant students". Reading and Writing: An Interdisciplinary Journal, 1973–1990, 2011.

However, Cummins argues that what could really promote the literacy development of those students, is helping them to affirm their identities through the use of L1 as a medium of instruction. By contrast, "encouraging them to assimilate linguistically by prohibiting them from using their home language within the school reinforces the stigma of belonging to a group perceived as inferior" (p. 1985)[13].

Many European countries give a lot of importance to the host country's language, which newcomers need to learn as soon as possible, paying very little attention to the languages of origin of migrants, because, as already said, they are often seen by speakers of dominant languages and by policy makers as obstacles to integration. But for a deep and real process of integration, policies and systems of education should not undervalue the importance of promoting and provide rights to immigrant languages, which will often maintain an important symbolic value for immigrant groups. As Cummins (2011)[14] states, respecting and assuring them much more dignity and esteem would allow every newcomer to feel accepted and free to express part of his/her own identity, instead of feeling judged or disadvantaged, and therefore forced to confine his/her self in a parallel ghettoised society. To avoid exclusion and ghettoisation, efforts should be made in order to elevate the prestige and esteem of IM, not only granting rights as those of regional minorities, but also promoting a widespread knowledge of them among the whole society. As Lo Bianco (2010)[15] stresses, this should be carried out by education ministries on a national level, who should be made aware of the importance of a multilingual education that gives importance to the maintenance and promotion of the IM languages. In other words, as Lo Bianco (2010)[16] states, "Critical awareness" should be developed in the society, aiming to contest the effects of negative characterization of the heritage language by dominant social and linguistic *milieu* and reinforcing a world-view that safeguards cultural diversity. Attaching a great importance to the maintenance of the language of origin does not anyway intend to diminish the value of learning the host society's language which is still of vital importance. But it must be kept in mind that "language learning roots integration in actual participation in the life of society: such language learning is not a precondition but rather an effect of the participation of migrants in the life of the new society" (Council of Europe 2008,

---

13 Ibid.
14 Ibid.
15 Lo Bianco, Joe. "The importance of language policies and multilingualism for cultural diversity", 2010, p. 56.
16 Ibid.

p. 15)[17]. Language skills, for instance, should not be a prerequisite to obtain a residence permission, since this in the long term will not guarantee any integration if there is no active involvement in the life of society, for instance, through cultural activities. In this regard, it must be kept in mind that, as the Council again states: "employing the host society's language and using several languages for communication is both the most direct form of inclusive socialisation and a "natural" form of language acquisition".

4 Conclusions

To sum up, after having analysed the factual attitude of the EU toward immigrant linguistic rights, it must be stated that such a disregard is not acceptable in a community that claims to be a multicultural and multilingual landscape. Especially taking into consideration the fact that the value of cultural diversity is stressed and granted for some minorities, it seems absurd not to extend those attentions also to IM. Over the past decades, Europe has experienced an extraordinary increase in migration, and in order to offer concrete responses to the present so-called immigration crisis, aiming toward a real process of integration, the importance of promoting a more balanced equality of those languages should be guaranteed, as the role of language in the process of integration is essential. The paper focused on the importance of the retention of IM languages, rather than on the host language learning and the ways to support and implement it, as the latter alone will not lead to a real process of integration. Succeeding in the former instead means recognizing the potential of language to be a container of human rights, equality and dignity and a multilingual education and approach to languages can be considered the means to create a real social inclusion. In order to respond to diversity in a positive way, the need for an intercultural dialogue in nowadays world is becoming more and more relevant. Intercultural dialogue is necessary to prevent marginalisation and discrimination, which can only lead to negative effects for everyone. The first element that must be taken into consideration is our common human dignity, which involves also respect for different cultural identities in all their components: food, language, religion and so on. Intercultural competences must be taught and learned, this is why the role of education is a fundamental one in ensuring the development of a positive attitude towards diversity in the future. In this regard the Council of the European

---

17 Council of Europe (2008). "The role of languages in policies for the integration of adult migrants". Concept paper by Jean-Claude Beacco, from: www.coe.int/t/dg4/linguistic/Publications_EN.asp, 2008.

Union states: "Education and training systems have to lead people to accept that racism and intolerance have no place in our society; that discrimination is unacceptable" (Coe, 2001, p. 13)[18]. Training the next generations' minds in respecting and accepting diversity and multilingualism as a normal state of affairs should be the aim of today's education ministries, which should therefore also move from the monolingual habit to a more inclusive attitude.

Bibliography

Council of Europe "Definition of Multilingualism", Language education Policy. n.d. retrieved 20.11.2017, from: www.coe.int/t/dg4/linguistic/Division_EN.asp#TopOfPage.

Council of Europe (1992). "European Charter of Minority Languages". Retrieved 08.03.2018, from: http://www.coe.int/it/web/conventions/fulllist/conventions/rms/090000168007c095.

Council of Europe (2008). "The Role of Languages in Policies for the Integration of Adult Migrants". Concept paper by Jean-Claude Beacco, retrieved 01.04.2018, from: www.coe.int/t/dg4/linguistic/Publications_EN.asp.

Council of the European Union (2001). "The Concrete Future Objectives of Education and Training Systems", Report from the Education Council to the European Council, 5980/01 EDUC 23, Brussels, 14.02.2001.

Cummins, J. (2011). "The intersection of cognitive and sociocultural factors in the development of reading comprehension among immigrant students". Reading and Writing: An Interdisciplinary Journal, 1973–1990, 13(8).

Eurobarometer (2012). Report: "Europeans and their languages". Retrieved 15.09.2018, from: http://ec.europa.eu/public_opinion/archives/ebs/ebs_386_en.pdf.

Extra, G. & Yagmur, K. (2004). Urban Multilingualism in Europe Immigrant Minority Languages at Home and School. Clevedon, Avon, England: Multilingual Matters.

Gogolin, I. (1997). "The monolingual habitus as the common feature in teaching in the language of the majority in different countries". Per Linguam 13(2), pp. 40–41.

Kloss, H. (1971). "Language rights and immigrant groups". International Migration Review 5, pp. 250–268.

---

18 Council of the European Union. "The concrete future objectives of education and training systems." Report from the Education Council to the European Council, 2001.

Kymlicka, W. (2001). "Politics in the Vernacular: Nationalism, Multiculturalism, and Citizenship", Oxford, Oxford University Press. Retrieved 10.08.2018, from: http://www.oxfordscholarship.com/view/10.1093/0199240981.001.00 01/acprof-9780199240982.

Lo Bianco, J. (2010). "The importance of language policies and multilingualism for cultural diversity". International Social Science Journal 61(199), 37–67.

Lo Bianco, J. (2013). "An Interview with Joseph Lo Bianco", retrieved 03.09.2018, from: www.channelviewpublications.wordpress.com/2013/08/06/ an-interview-with-joseph-lo-bianco/.

Nic Craith, M. (2006). Europe and the Politics of Language Citizens, Migrants and Outsiders. Basingstoke, UK, and New York: Palgrave Macmillan.

Rubio-Marín, R. (2003) "Exploring the Boundaries of Language Rights: Insiders, Newcomers, and Natives", in Nomos: Secession and new determination, JStor, pp. 136–173. Retrieved 22.11.2018, from: http://www.jstor.org/ stable/24220020.

III I diritti sospesi tra bisogno e desiderio

Enrico Battaglia, Marcella Cometti, Stefano Piccioni

Introduzione

Do you need it or do you want it? Quando parliamo di diritti parliamo di qualcosa di cui abbiamo effettivamente *bisogno* (rientrante, per cui, nella sfera del bisogno-essenziale) o di qualcosa che entra a far parte della sfera del *desiderio* che, non riconosciuto come imprescindibile, può essere soddisfatto secondariamente o accidentalmente?

In una società basata sul consumo e sul consumismo sfrenato, tendiamo non solo a confondere desideri e bisogni, ma anche a non riconoscere – accecati dai nostri "desideri individualisti" – il bisogno dell'Altro e a sopprimere i suoi desideri. Il dominante modo di vita consumistico, infatti, porta gli esseri umani a riconoscere gli "Altri" non come suoi pari bensì come oggetti di consumo; in quest'ottica tendiamo a giudicare l'Altro in base alla quantità di piacere che può offrire e in termini di "giustificazione economica dell'investimento"[1].

Nella società del consumo, dunque, non c'è più spazio per l'attenzione all'Altro in quanto diverso (e per questo unico) né, tantomeno, c'è tempo per volgere lo sguardo al *bisogno* e al *desiderio* che scaturisce dalle vite altrui. La solidarietà umana, intesa anche come interessamento al rispetto dei diritti e dei bisogni degli Altri, è la prima vittima dei trionfi del mercato dei consumi[2].

I tre scritti che seguono hanno l'intento di prendere in considerazione la tensione tra la sfera del bisogno e quella del desiderio con riferimento a specifici diritti della persona. L'idea è quella di fondere diverse discipline (design, diritto, psicologia e pedagogia) per indagare il contenuto di diritti che, sebbene

---

1 Zygmunt Bauman, *Amore Liquino*, Roma, ed. Laterza, 2003, pag. 105.
2 Zygmunt Bauman, *Amore Liquino*, Roma, ed. Laterza, 2003, pag. 106.

essenziali, rimangono troppo spesso relegati nella sfera del desiderio e non riconosciuti come bisogni effettivi delle persone. In generale, l'obiettivo dei quattro
contributi è quello di dimostrare che quando il bisogno dell'Altro entra nella
sfera del *desiderato*, questo non viene considerato nella sua intrinseca importanza: se, al contrario, si iniziasse a riconoscere e comprendere il desiderio
dell'Altro come bisogno da soddisfare -in quanto essenziale perché legato a
diritti fondamentali-, si inizierebbe a costruire un dialogo alla pari tra Noi e
l'Altro.

In *"Fuori di qui"* di Battaglia, la comunicazione e l'interesse a tematiche sociali
si coniugano con grafica ed arti visive: il design diventa qui strumento d'indagine
della condizione esistenziale e della situazione burocratica che i richiedenti asilo
si trovano a vivere ogni giorno nel nostro paese. Costoro si trovano a confrontarsi
costantemente con uno stato di sospensione non solo dei loro bisogni e desideri ma
anche dei loro diritti.

Come si può desumere dal contributo di Cometti (*"Il diritto al ricongiungimento familiare dei migranti beneficiari di protezione internazionale: un diritto che
rimane desiderio"*), tale situazione di aleatorietà non caratterizza solo le vite dei
richiedenti asilo ma anche quelle dei rifugiati e beneficiari di protezione sussidiaria
(cioè coloro che sono stati riconosciuti meritevoli di protezione da parte dello Stato
ospitante). Con riferimento al diritto all'unità familiare di queste persone, è suffi-
ciente indagare le prassi delle amministrazioni competenti ad attuare tale diritto,
per rendersi conto che il diritto-bisogno dei rifugiati a vivere con la propria famiglia
(coniuge e figli minori) viene sovente compromesso e catalogato come desiderio
a cui, solo occasionalmente, dare degno riconoscimento. Infatti se, da un lato, il
diritto internazionale, europeo e nazionale tutela il diritto del rifugiato a farsi raggiungere dai propri familiari nel Paese dove tale *status* è stato riconosciuto, dall'altro
egli dovrà interfacciarsi costantemente con ostacoli che rendono non effettivo tale
diritto: molteplici sono gli ostacoli che il rifugiato o la sua famiglia incontra per
ottenere il ricongiungimento e molteplici sono le ripercussioni della compressione
di tale diritto, in termini di salute psicofisica, vulnerabilità e processo di inclusione
sociale.

Infine, come argomentato da Piccioni in *"L'assistenza sessuale a persone con
disabilità: materiale pedagogico e strumento di cura"*, anche il diritto alla salute
sessuale (riconosciuto come uno dei diritti umani fondamentali dall'ordinamento internazionale, nonché da molti accordi universali) è un bisogno primario e primordiale, un'urgenza potentissima, spesso negata e sottovalutata con
riferimento a persone portatrici di disabilità. Essendo la sessualità uno degli
essenziali modi di espressione della persona umana, il diritto di disporne liberamente è, quindi, *"senza dubbio un diritto soggettivo assoluto, che va ricompreso*

*tra le posizioni soggettive direttamente tutelate dalla Costituzione ed inquadrato
tra i diritti inviolabili della persona umana che l'art. 2 Cost. impone di garantire"*[3].
Come si potrà osservare nella trattazione che segue, anche in questo caso
un diritto essenziale che nasce da un desiderio primario e primordiale, rimane
relegato – con specifico riferimento alle persone disabili – alla sfera del deside-
rio-tabù: l'opinione pubblica spegne i riflettori su quesiti che ci interrogano sul
nostro rapporto con la sfera emotiva e sessuale; che ci interrogano sulla nostra
morale, su quella della nostra cultura, del nostro contesto e del nostro paese.
Secondo le parole di Recalcati[4], il desiderio è "(…) una forza inconscia che
spinge alla relazione con l'Altro e che sempre implica un inciampo, uno sban-
damento, una perdita di padronanza. Non sono "io" che decido il mio desiderio,
è il desiderio che decide di me, mi rapisce e mi anima". Ecco dunque che se
la volontà è quella di costruire un "dialogo tra culture", altro non si deve fare
che continuare ad alimentare il *desiderio* dell'Altro (sia dello straniero che della
persona diversa da me in quanto portatore di disabilità), proprio in quanto è il
riconoscimento del desiderio dell'altro che spinge alla relazione.
Ma, come dimostrato anche dai tre contributi che seguiranno, fin tanto che la
politica, le amministrazioni e la società nel suo complesso hanno serie difficoltà
nel *riconoscere* il desiderio dell'Altro, un incontro in un rapporto di parità -e
quindi un dialogo- non sarà possibile.

---

3   sentenza Corte Cost., 18 dicembre 1987 n. 561.
4   Massimo Recalcati, *I ritratti del desiderio,* ed. Cortina Raffaello, 2012.

Enrico Battaglia

"Fuori di qui": il graphic journalism racconta la realtà sospensa dei richiedenti asilo in Italia

Abstract: "Fuori di qui" is an illustrated book about the bureaucratic situation and the existential condition of asylum seekers in Italy. In order to understand how to communicate properly this complex and precarious condition, the research considered many disciplines, embracing social, ethnographic and artistic approaches. As result, "Fuori di qui" describes the real experience of the everyday life of five asylum seekers who are living in a refugee shelter in the north-east of Italy. For a complete and adequate communication of this multifaced theme, the story is depicted from different points of view, which are recognizable from diffent graphic styles. This "graphic documentary" volume, is addressed to all those who are interested on this social theme and who would examin in depth some aspects of the everydaylife of refugees. The purpose of this volume is not to educate or influence the audience, but just giving the possibility to open reflections about an actual theme.

1 La sospensione esistenziale del richiedente asilo

Secondo la teologia il Limbo designa *"lo stato e il luogo dove si trovano dopo la vita coloro che sono morti con il solo debito del peccato originale: tali sono i bambini non battezzati e le persone in cui, per morbo o altro, non s'è mai svegliata la ragione, e sono morti così senza battesimo [...] la parola stessa dimostra la credenza che il limbo sia come un orlo eterno dell'inferno"*.[1]

Vivere il limbo significa vivere uno stato di sospensione esistenziale che tiene fermi gli individui che la stanno esperendo in uno stato di indeterminatezza, dubbio e attesa.

Nella contemporaneità spesso la sospensione induce le persone a vivere una fase di incertezza a causa di condizioni di tipo sociale e burocratico quali la precarietà lavorativa, la disoccupazione, o nei casi più gravi, la prigionia.

Attualmente la categoria che probabilmente sta vivendo con maggiore visibilità e problematicità all'interno della società odierna questo stato di sospensione sono i richiedenti asilo politico. Individui che perseguitati nel paese di origine

---

1   Treccani enciclopedie, Limbo (Accesso web il 17.03.2016 http://www.treccani.it/enciclopedia/limbo_%28Enciclopedia-Italiana%29/).

chiedono protezione ad un'altra autorità sovrana che dispone di un sistema di accoglienza specifico.[2]

Nella costituzione italiana viene stabilito che *"lo straniero, al quale sia impe-dito nel suo paese l'effettivo esercizio delle libertà democratiche, ha diritto d'asilo nel territorio della Repubblica, secondo le condizioni stabilite dalla legge".*[3]

Con riferimento al sistema di accoglienza italiano, che ancora è in fase di costruzione, la condizione in cui versano i richiedenti asilo rappresenta appieno l'idea di limbo e sospensione, in quanto sono costretti a vivere in una condizione incerta fino a che la loro domanda di asilo non verrà accolta.[4]

In questo stato di immobilismo sociale i richiedenti asilo si configurano, usando le parole di Alessandro Dal Lago (1999), come *non persone*, ossia indi-vidui ai quali viene revocato temporaneamente il proprio *background* sociale e culturale nelle transizioni ordinarie o nel linguaggio pubblico.[5]

La ricerca condotta, affronta la condizione esistenziale e burocratica che i richiedenti asilo politico si ritrovano a vivere ogni giorno all'interno del terri-torio italiano.

Tramite un approccio di tipo etnografico[6] dapprima, e grafico-artistico[7] poi, nasce "Fuori di qui", un volume illustrato che descrive un'esperienza reale vissuta nel nordest del paese all'interno di un CARA (Centro di Accoglienza per Richie-denti Asilo).

2   Ministero per l'interno, (2015) Centri per l'immigrazione (Accesso web il 25.05.2016 http://www.interno.gov.it/it/temi/immigrazione-e-asilo/sistema-accoglienza-sul-ter-ritorio/centri-immigrazione).
3   L' Articolo 10, Co.3, della Costituzione Italiana stabilisce che «L'ordinamento giuridico italiano si conforma alle norme del diritto internazionale generalmente riconosciute. La condizione giuridica dello straniero è regolata dalla legge in conformità delle norme e dei trattati internazionali. Lo straniero, al quale sia impedito nel suo paese l'effettivo esercizio delle libertà democratiche garantite dalla Costituzione italiana, ha diritto d'asilo nel territorio della Repubblica, secondo le condizioni stabilite dalla legge. Non è ammessa l'estradizione dello straniero per reati politici».
4   Liberti, S. (2016) Il sistema di accoglienza dei migranti in Italia è come una cipolla (Accesso web 25.05.2016 via http://www.internazionale.it/opinione/stefano-li-berti/2016/05/12/accoglienza-mi-granti-italia-cipolla).
5   Dal Lago, A. (1999). Non persone- L'esclusione dei migranti in una società globale. Milano: Feltrinelli.
6   Ronzon, F (2008). Sul campo. Breve guida alla pratica etnografica. Roma: Meltemi.
7   Eisner, W (1996). Graphic Storytelling and Visual Narrative. New York: W W Norton & Co Inc.

Nello specifico, all'interno della struttura d'accoglienza, l'inchiesta si è servita della pratica etnografica dell'osservazione partecipante[8], dalla quale è poi nata l'esigenza di creare un prodotto grafico che avesse come obiettivo quello di raccontare e rendere accessibile ad un pubblico più vasto, un tema che spesso per la specificità tecnica con la quale viene affrontato risulta difficilmente comprensibile.

Il prodotto editoriale eseguito, ascrivibile alla categoria del *Graphic Journalism,* documenta e narra dunque attraverso illustrazioni e parole l'esperienza diretta sul campo. Il volume[9] svela la condizione quotidiana di cinque giovani ragazzi che popolano uno di questi centri e le problematiche che si annidano all'interno di un sistema d'integrazione incerto e senza garanzie. Una situazione che grava pesantemente sui desideri e sui bisogni dei soggetti interessati.

Molteplici possono essere le considerazioni fini alla selezione di una casa di accoglienza rispetto a un'altra. Tuttavia, in un progetto che si avvale degli strumenti della comunicazione visiva, un criterio preponderante nella scelta del soggetto è sicuramente quello estetico.

Lo stesso paesaggio nel quale si colloca l'edificio scelto per questo studio si accorda al tema della sospensione: immerso nella campagna della pedemontana veneta comunica visivamente tematiche quali la solitudine, l'isolamento e la noia. Temi già ampiamente documentati nella storia dell'arte, che fornisce in questo contesto l'ispirazione necessaria nella scelta degli strumenti visivi e delle tecniche da adottare al fine di rappresentare al meglio questa condizione di sospensione esistenziale.

2 La sospensione nella cultura visiva

Non è la prima volta che le immagini disegnate narrano i migranti, e tra gli autori contemporanei più famosi vi è l'internazionale Joe Sacco. Considerato il pioniere di questo genere, con i suoi reportage a fumetti ha raccontato la situazione dell'ex-Jugoslavia, di Gaza e delle rotte clandestine tra nord Africa e Italia.[10] Più recentemente anche l'italiano Zero Calcare ha fatto rivivere ai lettori i tragici episodi della città assediata di Kobane al confine tra Turchia e Siria nel reportage umoristico Kobane Calling.[11] Entrambi gli autori nonostante la diversità nello stile affrontano questioni sensibili e complesse con grande lucidità.

---

8   Ronzon, F (2008). Sul campo. Breve guida alla pratica etnografica. Roma: Meltemi.
9   Battaglia, E (2016). Fuori di qui. Bolzano: Libera Università di Bolzano.
10 Sacco, J (2012) Reportages, Milano: Mondadori – Strada blu narrativa.
11 Zerocalcare (2016) Kobane calling. Milano: Bao Publishing.

In termini pratici la lettura e l'analisi dei testi di questi autori, hanno permesso con maggiore facilità la costruzione di Fuori di qui. Entrambi infatti, adottano alcuni accorgimenti visivi che facilitano la comprensione di tematiche di guerra che sono lontane per il cittadino europeo contemporaneo. La rappresentazione dei dettagli della vita di tutti i giorni dei protagonisti, come gli oggetti e gli affetti personali, aumentano la connessione emotiva del lettore e una conseguente identificazione. Gli autori evitano la stereotipizzazione della guerra, ma entrano nelle case dei personaggi, delineandone graficamente la quotidianità e le abitudini. Questi stratagemmi visivi, basati sui dettagli quotidiani sono stati di grande aiuto per illustrare una tematica come quella dell'immobilità all'interno di un centro di accoglienza.

Dando uno sguardo alla storia dell'arte, Edward Hopper e Giorgio De Chirico sono due validi esempi nella rappresentazione visiva dello spazio sospeso e del senso di attesa della vita quotidiana. Ascrivibili rispettivamente al realismo e al surrealismo, i due artisti nonostante operino su livelli stilistici differenti, condividono alcuni elementi visivi che li avvicinano fortemente. Entrambi nelle loro opere, infatti, usano un'architettura autoritaria e rigida, che tagliata da una luce carica di significato simbolico aumenta il senso di rarefazione circostante[12]. L'architettura rappresentata con forti chiaroscuri conferisce un senso di sospensione così potente da rendere una scena eterna.[13] Altro elemento importante è l'assenza di vita all'interno delle loro opere. Il paesaggio è disabitato o occupato da pochi individui, le cui azioni sono spesso inconcludenti e sembrano non avere un obiettivo. Questo senso di inettitudine non fa altro che aumentare l'atmosfera ovattata generale.

Concludendo, i due artisti rappresentano visivamente l'immobilità quotidiana attraverso la *non azione* accostata a potenti giochi di luce e ombra. Gli elementi estetico-visivi di questi autori diventano un valido esempio e punto di partenza nella progettazione di un lavoro editoriale che ha come tema centrale la sospensione.

Anche nella lettura di "Fuori di qui" si diventa spettatori di questa immobilità paesaggistica e umana.

---

12 s.a I luoghi dell'arte 6 (2003) – Nascita e sviluppi dell'arte del XX secolo. Roma: 2003 Electa.
13 s.a Giorgio De Chirico – Pictor Optimus. Milano: Rizzoli | Skira.

3 L'etnografia come metodo di indagine

Analizzando i lavori preesistenti nel campo del reportage grafico,[14] e del *visual journalism*[15] si è convenuto che il metodo migliore per parlare della sospensione esistenziale del richiedente asilo avvenisse attraverso l'etnografia.[16] Questa scelta è stata fatta in funzione della creazione di un prodotto di comunicazione visiva il più oggettivo possibile.

In un primo momento l'ipotesi era di costruire un rapporto con gli abitanti della casa basato sull'intervista. Insieme ai responsabili e agli operatori della struttura però si è preferito un altro approccio: l'osservazione partecipante.[17]

Questa tecnica prevede che il ricercatore-etnografo si stabilisca lentamente all'interno di un gruppo sociale. In questo modo, partecipando alle attività quotidiane, instaura dove possibile un rapporto di fiducia e di empatia. Diventando così mimetico, il ricercatore compie le dovute investigazioni mantenendo un buon equilibrio tra osservazione e partecipazione.

Con questa tecnica etnografica la dicotomia tra osservatore-osservato si dissolve lasciando spazio a dinamiche e meccanismi autentici, che con altri approcci invece potrebbero non emergere. Optare per questa tecnica ha cambiato dunque gli strumenti d'indagine: è stato eliminato qualsiasi supporto audiovisivo che potesse impedire la spontaneità e l'autenticità dell'esperienza, a favore di un diario fatto di parole e illustrazioni che potessero facilitare il processo di comprensione, catturando così impressioni ed esperienze.

In questo caso specifico gli ospiti del centro sono una decina. Questi ragazzi, con un'età compresa tra i 20 e 30 anni, vivono in una casa singola indipendente collocata in un piccolo complesso residenziale in un paesino della profonda campagna veneta.

Il centro per la sua posizione dunque non facilita il movimento dei ragazzi, ma anzi ne aumenta il senso d' isolamento. I beneficiari del centro infatti, ad eccezione di poche attività svolte all'esterno (principalmente i corsi di lingua italiana) sono indotti per questioni logistiche a trascorrere la maggior parte del tempo all'interno della struttura.

La possibilità di poter osservare direttamente i meccanismi quotidiani all'interno del centro, ha fornito la possibilità di testimoniare come la mancanza di

14 Zerocalcare (2016) Kobane calling. Milano: Bao Publishing.
15 Sacco, J (2012) Reportages, Milano: Mondadori – Strada blu narrativa.
16 Ronzon, F (2008). Sul campo. Breve guida alla pratica etnografica. Roma: Meltemi.
17 Ronzon, F (2008). Sul campo. Breve guida alla pratica etnografica. Roma: Meltemi.

operosità in cui versano i ragazzi accresca l'apatia, il senso di indolenza e la conseguente frustrazione.

Inizialmente l'approccio adottato si limitava all'osservazione degli spazi comuni della struttura e della quotidianità dei ragazzi al suo interno, in modo tale da instaurare un rapporto di fiducia e di conoscenza. Nel corso di pochi giorni questi spazi si sono trasformati in luoghi di collaborazione e condivisione, dove venivano svolte attività casalinghe e di svago: principalmente giardinaggio, pulizie domestiche, preparazione del cibo e giochi con il pallone, semplici attività che hanno gettato le basi per creare una relazione un po' più solida.

In un clima di continua attesa e indeterminatezza, questa tecnica si è rivelata estremamente favorevole sin dall'inizio. In queste condizioni, infatti, i ragazzi stessi hanno scelto, superate le prime incertezze, di aprirsi al nuovo ospite instaurando un rapporto che si è rivelato sinceramente profondo e significativo, oltre che utile ai fini della ricerca.

La scelta di adottare l'osservazione partecipante è stata avvalorata dall'attività riflessiva che il ricercatore ha fatto su di sé. Condividere la quotidianità all'interno di uno spazio circoscritto e multiculturale ha inevitabilmente scatenato una riflessione spontanea sulla varietà di usi e costumi, appartenenti e non, alla propria cultura, creando in questo modo un dialogo e un ribaltamento di prospettive. La ricerca, infatti, ha spesso cambiato il soggetto delle domande, trasformando a volte l'analisi in un'autoriflessione che ha indotto ad una maggiore empatia: "...e se a chiedere asilo politico fossimo noi?".

Questo costante capovolgimento tra noi e gli altri, facilitato dall'attività di scrittura del diario, ha permesso una continua riflessione sulla sospensione esistenziale come qualcosa che appartiene a tutti gli esseri umani.

Facendo leva dunque sulle sensazioni e sulle emozioni che questi stati di transizione provocano, si permette una maggiore comprensione della logorante attesa dei richiedenti asilo. Il processo d'immedesimazione risulta decisivo nella descrizione di un tema che solitamente è affrontato con estrema oggettività, perché permette una maggiore comprensione delle problematicità dell'altro.

La raccolta del materiale avveniva giornalmente, principalmente la sera quando tutte le attività quotidiane erano terminate. La ricerca sul campo è durata due mesi, dove sono stati raccolti 200 schizzi a mano libera con penna biro, e 103 pagine di diario e riflessioni su di un taccuino formato A5. Il materiale raccolto è composto principalmente da conversazioni, aneddoti, avvenimenti e impressioni quotidiane. Tutto ciò, si è rivelato estremamente utile nei mesi seguenti durante la progettazione del volume: consultare le memorie e i disegni ha facilitato la creazione della struttura narrativa, favorendo la precisione nel racconto dei fatti.

4 Risultati dell'osservazione partecipante

I ragazzi stessi, durante le varie attività quotidiane lamentavano il senso d'isolamento ed emarginazione all'interno del paese. Testimoniavano infatti l'assenza di cortesia da parte dei vicini o del piccolo bar di quartiere, e i pochi di loro che sapevano l'italiano avevano capito i testi dei cartelloni politici che tapezzavano il borgo. Alcune fazioni politiche, infatti, parafrasando le parole di Alessandro dal Lago, sono fortemente attaccate ai valori regionali, e non si rivelano sempre benevolenti nei confronti dello straniero. Anzi, spesso sfruttano ansie urbane che portano ad un incitamento all'ostilità nei suoi confronti.[18] Quest'atteggiamento porta i ragazzi a percepire un sentimento di sfiducia e colpa, che si trasforma nel tempo in demoralizzazione. Gli unici contatti con la popolazione autoctona avvengono all'interno delle attività promosse dal centro, dunque corsi di lingua, uscite di piacere o di carattere burocratico. Al di fuori quindi degli operatori, degli educatori e dei volontari i ragazzi hanno scarsamente la possibilità di intraprendere relazioni con gente locale. Questo significa che il sistema di riferimento è caratterizzato da un'indotta-autoindotta ghettizzazione dei richiedenti asilo, che sfavorisce già in partenza un futuro processo d'integrazione.

Queste problematiche inoltre, emerse durante le conversazioni con i professionisti operanti del centro, sono amplificate dal lento sistema burocratico con il quale i ragazzi si confrontano. Il richiedente asilo stipula infatti al suo arrivo un contratto di diritti e doveri con la prefettura e il centro di accoglienza, sottostando così a regolamenti statali (comuni a tutti i centri di accoglienza sul territorio italiano) e privati (gestiti territorialmente).[19] Per quanto riguarda le norme statali, nella pratica, questo contratto prevede una sorta di "libertà vigilata" basata per esempio sul rispetto di orari prestabiliti. Infatti, dalle ore 9:00 del mattino alle 20:00 di sera i ragazzi del centro sono liberi di muoversi all'esterno della struttura, allo scadere del coprifuoco devono trovarsi in casa, e ciò è tasssativo. La gestione delle pulizie, l'approvvigionamento dei viveri e l'organizzazione delle attività giornaliere, è normato privatamente dalla struttura.

La burocrazia regola dunque in toto la condizione quotidiana dei rifugiati, che vivono quella che a tutti gli effetti si presenta come una logorante attesa in

---

18 Dal Lago, A. (1999). Non persone- L'esclusione dei migranti in una società globale. Milano: Feltrinelli.

19 Ministero per l'interno, (2015) Centri per l'immigrazione (Accesso web il 25.05.2016 http://www.interno.gov.it/it/temi/immigrazione-e-asilo/sistema-accoglienza-sul-territorio/centri-immigrazione).

semilibertà. Alcuni dei ragazzi del centro possono infatti confermare la snervante attesa (nel loro caso prolungata a 18 mesi) dei documenti richiesti.

"Pensa che a volte sono così annoiato, che vado da camera a cucina, poi di nuovo a camera, e così continuo per anche pomeriggio intero… così senza motivo. Il tempo qui è senza fine, non guardo più ora [...] il tempo degli altri serve a me per capire mio tempo."[20]

Una situazione come questa esaspera i sentimenti degli ospiti del centro, che si riconoscono frustrati ed emotivamente demoliti, mettendo in dubbio a volte quei desideri e bisogni che gli hanno spinti a lasciare il paese di origine. La loro speranza iniziale è spazzata via e sostituita da rabbia e rancore: sentimenti talvolta pericolosi.

"Io un po' triste. Ho apena avuto notizia da comisione che ho ricevuto diniego. Non hano acetato richiesta mia di asilo. Loro hano deto che non hano dato documenti a me perchè non hanno capito perchè da sunnita sono diventato sciita. Ma perchè non hano chiesto? Io avrei risposto loro questo."[21]

La sofferenza emotiva generalizzata, è amplificata dalle dinamiche stesse che si creano tra i richiedenti. Si può costatare, infatti, che la convivenza forzata crea dissapori che sfociano talvolta in forme di gerarchizzazione e scontro.

"Io non voglio più stare con Alì, siamo diversi. Amico, il rispeto è prima cosa, bisogna rispetare le gerarchie. E lui non fa niente in questa casa, lui solo comandare. Ma amico sai cosa ti dico?
Posiamo stare lontani, vivere con gente che non è uguale a te no facile. Se poi durante giorno fai niente come noi, diventa inferno."[22]

5 Materiali e metodi nella costruzione del volume grafico

Alla luce di quanto esposto sopra, del materiale raccolto e della necessità di imporre un profondo senso di sospensione nel lettore, la stessa costruzione del libro ha richiesto accorgimenti particolari.

Nella sua componente narrativa "Fuori di qui" è caratterizzato da molteplici punti di vista. Uno descrittivo dove si dipana la narrazione principale, caratterizzato da testi blu, uno soggettivo che corrisponde al diario personale di chi ha

---

20 Battaglia, E (2016). Fuori di qui. Bolzano: Libera Università di Bolzano. Testimonianza di Abiodum.
21 Battaglia, E (2016). Fuori di qui. Bolzano: Libera Università di Bolzano. Testimonianza di Hamed.
22 Battaglia, E (2016). Fuori di qui. Bolzano: Libera Università di Bolzano. Testimonianza di Abiodum.

svolto la ricerca, caratterizzato da testi rossi, e uno burocratico che si trova a fine libro che raccoglie leggi ed articoli inerenti a diritti e doveri dei richiedenti asilo.

La scelta di dividere il libro in più blocchi narrativi è dettata dalla necessità di indurre nel lettore l'immedesimazione verso il narratore ed i personaggi e percepire l'oggettività distaccata della burocrazia in questo contesto.

La progettazione grafica svolge poi un ruolo essenziale nell'evocazione della sospensione.

Le illustrazioni realizzate a china, dal tratto irregolare e scomposto rappresentano i volti dei ragazzi del centro, gli spazi nei quali si muovono, oggetti e azioni quotidiane e scene personali del passato (in primis scontri armati, la famiglia e il viaggio verso l'Europa).

I colori scelti richiamano lo stesso schema adottato nei testi e pertanto i colori rosso e blu sono gli unici presenti. La scelta di questi due colori non è casuale: rosso e blu creano contrasto tra loro. Il colore blu, freddo, nella tradizione pittorica è infatti associato al limbo,[23] mentre il rosso è un colore caldo, sanguigno, e inevitabilmente legato alla sfera emotiva.

Pagine bianche si alternano inoltre a pagine scritte o illustrate, immagini a tutta pagina si contrappongono a miniature immerse nel vuoto. Anche questo gioco tra pieni e vuoti si impone all'interno dello *storytelling* e contribuisce a scandire il ritmo narrativo. Il lettore è così indirettamente portato a seguire momenti carichi di eventi e tensione emotiva grazie a pagine fittamente illustrate, e indotto alla riflessione dal vuoto grafico.

Altre scelte stilistiche contribuiscono a far percepire il lento fluire del tempo ed il senso di attesa nella lettura di "Fuori di qui". Alcuni fogli sono infatti piegati ed il lettore deve aprirli per leggerne il contenuto, inoltre i numeri di pagina sono deliberatamente assenti in tutto il libro, eccezion fatta per la parte finale che corrisponde al punto di vista burocratico, lontano dalla vita dei personaggi e unico inquadrabile in un arco temporale scandito.

In questa maniera indiretta ed inconscia il lettore è vittima del tempo come i personaggi del libro, sfogliare questo volume diventa pertanto un'esperienza fisica di attesa e impazienza.

Questo libro, toccando diversi aspetti della vita dei ragazzi, dovrebbe indurre il lettore alla comprensione dell'argomento nella sua complessità stimolandone la riflessione e il sentimento di solidarietà.

---

23 s.a I luoghi dell'arte 6 (2003) – Nascita e sviluppi dell'arte del XX secolo. Roma: 2003 Electa.

La progettazione grafica diventa il veicolo attraverso il quale comunicare complessi temi sociali con prodotti semplici ma efficaci.

In questo caso, com'è stato più volte enunciato, il libro realizzato diventa uno strumento per comunicare un'esperienza reale in un contesto sociale specifico.

6 Conclusioni

La ricerca effettuata vuole essere testimonianza della condizione vissuta dai richiedenti asilo in una piccola realtà italiana, paragonabile a tante presenti su suolo nazionale. In questo contesto si evince come i desideri e le speranze che hanno spinto queste persone ad intraprendere un lungo percorso verso migliori condizioni di vita si infrangano contro la realtà del sistema di accoglienza italiano, portando i protagonisti a vivere in una condizione logorante di sospensione esistenziale.

Se il richiedente asilo infatti si attende un immediato inserimento nella società italiana, fatto per esempio di interazioni con la popolazione locale e dalla possibilità di svolgere una qualche occupazione, si ritrova invece a sperimentare un sentimento di isolamento ed attesa continuo determinato dai lunghi tempi burocratici imposti dalla legge.

È evidente come la legge imponga una gestione inadeguata della quotidianità dei richiedenti asilo perché non basata sulle reali necessità e sui bisogni degli individui ma esclusivamente su obblighi e limiti.

L'isolamento testimoniato dai ragazzi, associato alla convivenza forzata tra individui appartenenti a realtà culturali differenti (non sempre conciliabili tra loro) crea un malcontento diffuso che fa della multiculturalità un rischio piuttosto che una virtù, e contribuisce a comprometterne l'integrazione in società. [24]

La condizione di sospensione esistenziale sperimentata dai richiedenti asilo si configura per tanto come una condizione di non appartenenza alla società. Chi la sperimenta è infatti escluso da qualsiasi processo che abbia a che vedere con la sua costruzione e partecipazione, e dalla possibilità dunque di soggettivarsi.

In questo contesto "Fuori di qui" getta le basi per un dialogo tra culture perché in grado di innescare nel lettore una riflessione sulle condizioni sperimentate dai richiedenti asilo in Italia, spingendo a sentimenti di immedesimazione e di solidarietà verso i protagonisti delle testimonianze raccolte.

---

24 Melting Pot, (2007) I limiti dei diritti umani: l'esempio emblematico del diritto d'asilo, (Accesso web il 27.05.2016 http://www.meltingpot.org/I-limiti-dei-diritti-umani-l-e-sempio-emblematico del.html#.WZqv6DNaZPM)

"Fuori di qui" si prefigura quindi di coprire un vuoto all'interno di un mercato editoriale in cui l'inchiesta grafica riscuote sempre più interesse, sia per come sono affrontati i contenuti e le tematiche, sia per la maniera con la quale verrebbero fruiti da un ipotetico lettore.

Bibliografia

Battaglia, E.: Fuori di qui. Bolzano. Stampato presso la Libera Università di Bolzano: Bolzano 2016.

Bora, G. et al: I luoghi dell'arte 6 – Nascita e sviluppi dell'arte del XX secolo. Electa: Roma 2003.

Dal Lago, A.: Non persone- L'esclusione dei migranti in una società globale. Feltrinelli: Milano 1999.

Eisner, W.: Graphic Storytelling and Visual Narrative. W W Norton & Co Inc: New York 1996.

Giorgio De Chirico: Pictor Optimus. Rizzoli | Skira Milano: 2005.

Liberti, S.: Il sistema di accoglienza dei migranti in Italia è come una cipolla, 2016. (Accesso web 25.05.2016 via http://www.internazionale.it/opinione/ stefano-liberti/2016/05/12/accoglienza-mi-granti-italia-cipolla)

Melting Pot: I limiti dei diritti umani: l'esempio emblematico del diritto d'asilo, 2007. (Accesso web il 27.05.2016 http://www.meltingpot.org/I-limiti-dei-diritti-umani-l-esempio-emblematico del.html#.WZqv6DNaZPM)

Ministero per l'interno: Centri per l'immigrazione 2015. (Accesso web il 25.05.2016 http://www.interno.gov.it/it/temi/immigrazione-e-asilo/sistema-accoglienza-sul-territorio/centri-immigrazione)

Ronzon, F.: Sul campo. Breve guida alla pratica etnografica. Meltemi: Roma 2008.

Rosi, G.: Fuocoammare. Istituto luce: Roma 2016.

Sacco, J.: Reportages, Mondadori – Strada blu narrativa: Milano 2012.

Treccani enciclopedie, Limbo (Accesso web il 17.03.2016 http://www.treccani.it/ enciclopedia/limbo_%28Enciclopedia-Italiana%29/)

Zerocalcare: Kobane calling. Bao Publishing: Milano 2016.

Marcella Cometti

Il diritto al ricongiungimento familiare dei migranti beneficiari di protezione internazionale: un diritto che rimane desiderio

Abstract: Family reunification is an entry channel enabling those who already reside legally in a Member State (referred to as sponsors) to be joined by their family members.It is widely recognized that family life is essential for the well-being of individuals and societies. For people fleeing war and persecution being reunited with their family members is generally their first priority upon arrival in the host country[1].The idea of analysing the problems that arise for beneficiaries of international protection concerning the possibility of family reunification, arose in order to understand which answers Europe might be able to give in addressing the current humanitarian crisis. Indeed, as long as the EU does not manage to guarantee a right to family reunification to such persons, it will not be possible to find a solution to the current difficulties in the management of migration flows.In this regard, nowadays, the idea that seems to guide the European Union's policy and several Member States is to limit not only *illegal immigration channels* (for example, through the controversial agreement between the EU and Turkey on 18 March 2016), but also *legal migration channel*, such as family reunification, that is the main channel of access to the European Union from third countries.The aim of the paper is to analyse specific problems faced by beneficiaries of international protection and their family members during the family reunification procedure and to understand how, these problems lead to a suspension of the desire-need of these people and to a perpetual and lasting state of "temporariness".Through an analysis of Italian and European legislation, the article aims to demonstrate that one of the goals of governments is not to encourage the refugees' integration. Indeed, it seems that the goal of governments is to make "suspended" the lives of beneficiaries of international, simply denying their right to family unity.

1 Introduzione

Il *Leitmotiv* che, negli ultimi tempi, muove l'Unione europea e gli Stati membri sembra essere quello di utilizzare ogni mezzo possibile per arrestare un processo migratorio che è in atto ormai da anni e, nei confronti del quale, ancora non si sono riuscite a prendere azioni strutturali e a lungo termine. La politica

---

1 Red Cross EU office, Ecre, *Distrupted flight, the realities of separated refugee families in the EU*, 2014.

migratoria europea sembra non essere ancora pronta ad accettare il fatto che l'immigrazione non costituisce un evento temporaneo, che può essere circoscritto in termini tali da non produrre alterazioni o contaminazioni con l'assetto sociale e culturale del paese ospitante, ma rappresenta una realtà permanente.

Per questo motivo gli Stati dell'Unione europea investono risorse per attuare politiche di "protezionismo allargato", di sicurezza e controllo sociale, invece di garantire il benessere e l'inserimento sociale degli immigrati già presenti sul territorio attraverso politiche di integrazione.

Queste politiche altro non sono che la conseguenza di un diffuso senso di insicurezza quotidiana che è insita nelle condizioni di vita di fasce sempre più ampie di popolazione. Questa insicurezza porta acqua al mulino dei politici come meglio si potrebbe: i governi non hanno interesse a placare le ansie dei loro cittadini bensì a dirottare l'ansia dai problemi che i governi non sanno risolvere (disponibilità di posti di lavoro, affidabilità e stabilità delle posizioni sociali, efficace protezione contro l'umiliazione sociale e la negazione della dignità, …) ad altri problemi, come quello dell'immigrazione[2]. Quello che la politica e, conseguentemente, le nuove normative assicurano non è altro che la promessa di rendere altrettanto insicure e *sospese* le vite dei migranti che giungono al nostro Paese.

Perciò, in particolare per i migranti che riescono[3] a fare domanda di protezione internazionale, inizia un processo che possiamo definire di continua tensione tra *bisogno* e *desiderio*[4] (ossia un processo dove il *bisogno* rimane solo desiderio che, raramente, verrà riconosciuto e compreso – dalla "società di accoglienza/ospitante", dalla politica, dal legislatore – come bisogno).

Così, anche laddove i diritti fondamentali di queste persone vengono apparentemente tutelati, nella prassi il migrante è costretto ad interfacciarsi

2 Zygmunt Bauman, *Stranieri alle porte*, Roma, ed. Laterza, 2016, pag. 26.
3 Si noti bene che il termine "riescono" non è casuale: secondo la nuova linea politica (e, tra pochi mesi, normativa) europea, la possibilità-diritto di presentare domanda di protezione internazionale in uno degli Stati membri non deve essere più data per scontata. Si fa qui riferimento sia volontà di "esternalizzazione del diritto di asilo" sia al c.d. approccio *hotspot* o *punto di crisi*, luogo di "scrematura" tra coloro che vogliono presentare domanda di asilo e coloro che, in una situazione di estrema fragilità psicologica, dichiarano nel Foglio Notizie di essere c.d. migranti economici. Il sistema dei *punti di crisi* si accompagna alla politica di *esternalizzazione del diritto d'asilo* che ha avuto il suo formale avvio con l'accordo UE – Turchia del 18 marzo 2016.
4 A questo proposito si veda *"Fuori di qui": il graphic journalism racconta la realtà sospesa dei richiedenti asilo in Italia*, Enrico Battaglia.

costantemente con ostacoli burocratici creati ad hoc affinché, nell'effettivo, non possa far valere tali diritti. Solo a titolo di esempio: i richiedenti protezione internazionale hanno diritto all'iscrizione anagrafica[5] che è, peraltro, presupposto per il rilascio della carta d'identità.

In Italia, l'iscrizione alle liste anagrafiche afferisce al diritto costituzionale di circolare e soggiornare liberamente sul territorio nazionale (art. 16 Cost.) e nel contempo è requisito essenziale per poter effettivamente esercitare altri diritti fondamentali[6]. Su tutto il territorio italiano, d'altro canto, si riscontrano prassi assolutamente illegittime messe in atto dagli Uffici dell'Anagrafe[7] i quali, con modalità più che arbitrarie, non consentono l'iscrizione dei richiedenti asilo -o la riconoscono ma a condizioni non previste nei testi di legge- sebbene tale diritto sia riconosciuto in svariati atti normativi e ministeriali[8].

Questo fenomeno di scollamento tra tutela normativa dei diritti fondamentali e prassi attuate nella realtà di tutti i giorni è chiaramente visibile anche con riferimento alla tutela del diritto all'unità familiare.

Nelle pagine che seguono si proverà ad indagare in che modo, rispetto alla tutela del diritto all'unità familiare, si concretizza tale scollamento e come questo porta ad una *sospensione* del desiderio-bisogno di tali persone e ad un perpetuo e duraturo stato di *temporaneità*.

---

5   Sul diritto all'iscrizione anagrafica dei richiedenti protezione internazionale: *Linee guida sul diritto alla residenza dei richiedenti e beneficiari di protezione internazionale* (SPRAR, Ministero dell'Interno, UNHCR, ANUSCA, ASGI) dicembre 2014; *art. 5 Regolamento Anagrafico d.p.r. 223/89; art. 5 D.Lgs. n. 142/2015; art. 6 co. 7 del D.Lgs. n. 286/1998 (T.U. Immigrazione).*

6   *Linee guida sul diritto alla residenza dei richiedenti e beneficiari di protezione internazionale* (SPRAR, Ministero dell'Interno, UNHCR, ANUSCA, ASGI), dicembre 2014.

7   A questo proposito, solo a titolo di esempio si vedano: https://www.asgi.it/notizie/asilo-prassi-illegittime-iscrizione-anagrafica-lettera-asgi/; https://www.asgi.it/notizie/a-seguito-della-segnalazione-effettuata-da-asgi-e-fondazione-guido-piccini-per-i-diritti-delluomo-onlus-unar-invita-il-comune-di-borgo-san-giacomo-bs-a-revocare-due-delibere-discriminatorie-e-il/; http://www.meltingpot.org/Asilo-e-prassi-illegittime-nell-iscrizione-anagrafica-in-21519.html#.WjA8iLpFzIU.

8   Art. 6 co. 7 del D.Lgs. n. 286/1998; art. 5 Regolamento Anagrafico d.p.r. 223/89; art. 5 D.Lgs. n. 142/2015; circolari del Ministero dell'Interno n. 8/1995, n. 2/1997; circolare del Ministero dell'Interno, Dipartimento per le Libertà Civili e l'Immigrazione del 18.05.2015 e del 17.08.2016.

2 Il ricongiungimento familiare dei beneficiari di protezione internazionale

Lo stato di *sospensione* dei diritti dei richiedenti e beneficiari di protezione internazionale è costante e voluto non solo dai governi ma anche dalle leggi che regolamentano l'esistenza dei migranti. Ad esempio il d.lgs. 25/2008 (c.d. Decreto Procedure) prevede che la Commissione Territoriale per il riconoscimento della protezione internazionale debba provvedere al colloquio del richiedente entro 30 giorni dalla presentazione della domanda e debba decidere entro i 3 giorni feriali successivi[9].

Quello che accade nella realtà invece è che, proprio perché i termini indicati dalla legge sono c.d. termini ordinatori[10], i richiedenti asilo attendono tra i 6 e i 12 mesi[11] -fino ad un massimo di 18 mesi- prima di essere uditi dalla competente Commissione. Tale attesa risulta estenuante in quanto la decisione che verrà presa determinerà se tali persone avranno diritto ad una vita passata alla luce del giorno o, in caso di esito negativo, esse dovranno sprofondare nell'ombra di un'esistenza fragile ed erratica[12].

Questo stato di *intermediatezza incarnata*[13] si ritrova, nello specifico, con riferimento al diritto al ricongiungimento familiare, oggetto della trattazione. Il diritto al ricongiungimento familiare consiste nella possibilità per gli stranieri che risiedono legalmente in uno Stato di farsi raggiungere dai propri familiari provenienti da Paesi terzi.

---

9   Art 27 d.lgs. 25/2008.
10 Un termine viene così detto se alla sua inosservanza, non sono previste sanzioni o effetti sfavorevoli.
11 Si vedano le statistiche fornite da Meltingpot, (http://www.meltingpot.org/IMG/pdf/ La_procedura_di_asilo_tra_norma_e_prassi.pdf), 17.06.2016.
12 Le persone a cui è stato negato l'asilo, infatti, per lo più rimangono in Europa e non sono oggetto di rimpatrio. Si veda a questo proposito un articolo di Daniela Sala, OpenMigration: "il numero dei rimpatri sia volontari che forzati fosse troppo basso. Nel 2016 i fogli di via emessi dagli stati membri dell'Unione Europea sono stati 489.055. Le persone effettivamente rimpatriate sono state circa la metà: 245.275 (il 17 per cento in più rispetto al 2015), di cui 75.815 rimpatriate dalla sola Germania, principalmente verso Albania e Serbia", http://openmigration.org/analisi/dove-finiscono-le-persone-a-cui-e-stato-negato-lasilo/.
13 Così viene definito lo *status* dei rifugiati anche da Bauman in "Amore Liquido", pag. 202: "nella condizione dei rifugiati, lo stato designato come *intermediatezza* incarnata si estende all'infinito (…)".
    Zygmunt Bauman, *Amore Liquido*, Roma, Ed. Laterza, 2003.

In tal caso, lo stato di *indeterminatezza*, di tensione *bisogno-desiderio*, si estrinseca in una situazione nella quale il *bisogno* del rifugiato[14] di vivere assieme alla sua famiglia nel Paese in cui tale status viene riconosciuto, rimane nella sfera del *desiderio* o, con altre parole, del *bisogno a cui non viene data la necessaria tutela*.

Studi[15] testimoniano l'impatto negativo che la separazione dalla famiglia ha, in particolar modo, sulle persone che ottengono la protezione internazionale e come questo influenzi la loro possibilità di integrazione nei Paesi in cui risiedono. Infatti, la costante preoccupazione rispetto ai familiari che hanno lasciato nel loro Stato d'origine, e l'assenza di una famiglia che possa dare loro supporto nel Paese ospite, accresce la loro vulnerabilità, quando già sono stati esposti ad esperienze traumatiche associate alla migrazione forzata. La separazione familiare tende ad essere associata a fragilità psicologica, che ha un impatto decisivo sulle abilità delle persone ad imparare la lingua, cercare lavoro, o semplicemente interagire con gli altri (inclusi gli ufficiali delle pubbliche amministrazioni).

Sebbene tali ricerche mostrano le ripercussioni negative conseguenti alla lontananza dei familiari, questa specifica categoria di persone ha serie difficoltà a fare in modo che i propri familiari li possano raggiungere "in sicurezza" nel Paese europeo dove tale protezione è stata accordata[16].

Infatti se, da un lato, il diritto internazionale (Convenzione di New York sui diritti del fanciullo del 20 novembre 1989[17], Convenzione europea dei diritti

---

14 Più precisamente il *bisogno* non solo del rifugiato ma anche del beneficiario di protezione sussidiaria o di protezione umanitaria.

15 B. McDonald-Wilmsen, S.M. Gifford, Refugee Resettlement, Family Separation and Australia's Humanitarian Programme. New Issues in Refugee Research, Research Paper No. 178, Geneva: United Nations High Commissioner for Refugees, 2009; 172 Red Cross EU office, Ecre, Disrupted flight, the realities of separated refugee families in the EU, 2014.

16 Si vedano, a questo proposito, le recenti modifiche introdotte nella normativa danese che hanno la finalità di limitare il diritto al ricongiungimento familiare dei beneficiari di protezione sussidiaria temporanea (legge L87 del 26.01.2016, contenente modifiche al Danish Aliens Act -"Udlændingeloven"-).
In Germania, il 25 Febbraio 2016, il Bundestag ha approvato il c.d. "Asylum Package II" che, tra l'altro, sospende la possibilità per i beneficiari di protezione sussidiaria di chiedere il ricongiungimento familiare per un periodo di due anni. Infine, in Austria il 27 aprile 2016, sono state approvate dal parlamento modifiche all'Asylgesetz del 2005 tra le quali viene inserito un limite di 3 anni per i beneficiari di protezione sussidiaria prima che questi possano fare domanda di ricongiungimento familiare.

17 Sebbene non imponga un diritto al ricongiungimento familiare, indirettamente in varie disposizioni ne richiede il riconoscimento al fine di tutelare i diritti del minore (art. 8, art. 9, art. 10).

dell'uomo e delle libertà fondamentali[18]), europeo (direttiva 2003/86, capo V) e nazionale (d.lgs. 286/1998, art 29 bis) tutela il diritto del rifugiato a farsi raggiungere dai propri familiari nel Paese dove tale *status* è stato riconosciuto, dall'altro egli dovrà interfacciarsi costantemente con ostacoli che rendono non effettivo tale diritto. A seguire ci si soffermerà su due dei *principali ostacoli* che, nell'ordinamento italiano, il rifugiato o la sua famiglia incontra per ottenere il ricongiungimento famigliare e su quelle che sono le *ripercussioni della compressione di tale diritto*, in termini di salute psicofisica, vulnerabilità e processo di inclusione sociale.

2.1 La c.d. famiglia ricongiunta: il diritto alla vita familiare dello straniero come "brutta copia" del diritto alla vita familiare goduta dal cittadino

Anzitutto, sempre facendo riferimento alla volontà di rendere le vite di queste persone *sospese* e senza necessari *punti di riferimento* (in questo caso familiari), sembra interessante notare come il diritto al ricongiungimento familiare dei cittadini non europei ha dato vita ad una nuova tipologia di famiglia: la c.d. famiglia ricongiunta.

La definizione di *famiglia ricongiunta*, corrispondente al concetto di *famiglia nucleare*[19] -coniuge e figli minori-, si discosta sia dalla tradizionale idea di famiglia propria dei paesi che costituiscono l'Unione, sia dall'idea di famiglia presente nei paesi d'origine di coloro che si avvalgono di tale diritto.

A proposito della differenza tra queste tipologie di famiglie "riconosciute" dalla legge nazionale ed europea, si può notare come la differenza più significativa riscontrabile tra le due fattispecie di ricongiungimento – rispettivamente dei cittadini europei ed extraeuropei – consta in primis nella definizione dei componenti della famiglia ricongiungibile: mentre la direttiva 2003/86 (relativa al ricongiungimento dei cittadini extraeuropei) garantisce il ricongiungimento solo con i membri della *famiglia nucleare*, l'articolo 2 della direttiva 2004/38

---

18 Di particolare rilievo ai fini della tutela della vita familiare sono l'articolo 8 e 12 della CEDU; l'articolo 12 è dedicato alla protezione del diritto di sposarsi e di costituire una famiglia, mentre l'articolo 8 alla tutela del rispetto della vita familiare (come anche alla tutela della vita privata, del domicilio e della corrispondenza).

19 Sulla definizione di famiglia nucleare si veda: Annual tripartite consultations on resettlement Geneva, 20–21 June 2001, Background Note for the Agenda Item: Family Reunification in the Context of Resettlement and Integration, Protecting the Family: Challenges in Implementing Policy in the Resettlement Context.

(relativa al ricongiungimento dei cittadini europei) fa riferimento ad una definizione di *famiglia "allargata"*[20].

Perciò, per gli per i beneficiari di protezione internazionale (o, più in generale, per tutti i cittadini extraeuropei) il ricongiungimento con altri familiari,
al di fuori di coniuge e figli minori non sposati, rimane un'eccezione (art. 29
co 1 d.lgs. 286/1998[21]) e non vengono tenute in considerazione da parte degli
Stati ospitanti le particolari situazioni in cui si trovano i rifugiati; ciò che viene
completamente sottovalutato sono i profondi cambiamenti della struttura familiare, che è il risultato delle migrazioni forzate, come, ad esempio, il fatto che una
famiglia sia composta da bambini di genitori che sono morti o scomparsi come
risultato di una guerra nel Paese d'origine o del viaggio che tali persone sono
costrette ad affrontare[22].

A questo proposito si consideri che paradossale sembra essere la situazione
(prevista da normativa europea ed italiana) per cui il minore straniero non
accompagnato, riconosciuto rifugiato in Italia, può chiedere ed ottenere il ricongiungimento con i genitori ma non con le sorelle-fratelli che si trovano, anch'essi,
nel Paese d'origine o di transito. Ciò, inevitabilmente, comporta una lesione del
principio di effettività del diritto dell'unità familiare in quanto, in tal modo, il

---

20 Ai fini della Direttiva, infatti, rientrano nella definizione di familiare: a) il coniuge; b)
il partner che abbia contratto con il cittadino europeo un'unione registrata sulla base
della legislazione di uno Stato membro; c) i discendenti diretti di età inferiore a 21 anni
o a carico e quelli del coniuge o partner di cui alla lettera b); d) gli ascendenti diretti
a carico e quelli del coniuge o partner di cui alla lettera b) e, per di più, la Direttiva,
sebbene non lo qualifichi come "familiare", prende in considerazione anche "il partner
con cui il cittadino dell'Unione abbia una relazione stabile 53 debitamente attestata"
(art. 3, c. 2, lett. b).

21 1. Lo straniero può chiedere il ricongiungimento per i seguenti familiari:

   a) coniuge non legalmente separato e di età non inferiore ai diciotto anni;
   b) figli minori, anche del coniuge o nati fuori del matrimonio, non coniugati, a condizione che l'altro genitore, qualora esistente, abbia dato il suo consenso;
   c) figli maggiorenni a carico, qualora per ragioni oggettive non possano provvedere
   alle proprie indispensabili esigenze di vita in ragione del loro stato di salute che
   comporti invalidità totale;
   d) genitori a carico, qualora non abbiano altri figli nel Paese di origine o di prove-
   nienza, ovvero genitori ultrasessantacinquenni, qualora gli altri figli siano impos-
   sibilitati al loro sostentamento per documentati, gravi motivi di salute.

22 Submission from the ECRE in response to the Commission's Green Paper on the
right to family reunification of third-country nationals living in the European Union
(Directive 2003/86/EC), pag. 5.

genitore viene messo di fronte alla scelta se lasciare gli altri figli nel Paese d'origine o di transito o, al contrario, non beneficiare del ricongiungimento.

Ancora: la Polonia[23], nel recepire la Direttiva 2003/86, non si è avvalsa della facoltà prevista dall'articolo 10.2[24]. Il ricongiungimento per il rifugiato è così riconosciuto solo con il coniuge e il figlio minorenne non sposato, senza che vi sia spazio per una valutazione caso per caso.

Un caso esaminato dal Report del Red Cross EU Office e di Ecre è quello di un siriano, al quale è stato riconosciuto lo status di rifugiato in Polonia, che ha chiesto il ricongiungimento familiare con moglie e figlio. Le altre due figlie erano maggiorenni e, per questo, non potevano beneficiare del ricongiungimento. La famiglia, una volta ottenuto il ricongiungimento, decise comunque di non beneficiarne, visto che, in tal modo avrebbero lasciato le due figlie non sposate da sole in Siria. Le autorità polacche non hanno tenuto in alcun modo in considerazione la situazione esistente in Siria[25].

Sicuramente questa nuova categoria di rapporto familiare, ossia la c.d. famiglia ricongiunta, nasce dalla necessità di bilanciare i vari interessi in gioco, ossia quello dei Paesi membri a mantenere il controllo sull'ingresso e il soggiorno di stranieri sul loro territorio e quello dell'unità familiare di coloro che, non cittadini, si ritrovano a soggiornare legalmente sul territorio di questi stessi Stati. È conseguenza di tale necessario bilanciamento il fatto che la famiglia ricongiunta vada a coincidere (con riferimento al ricongiungimento familiare dei cittadini extraeuropei) con la cosiddetta "famiglia nucleare".

D'altro canto, in tal modo, il diritto alla vita familiare che può essere goduto dallo straniero attraverso il ricongiungimento non è altro che una "brutta copia"

---

23 Red Cross EU office, Ecre, *Distrupted flight, the realities of separated refugee families in the EU*, pag. 11.

24 Art. 10.2 direttiva 2003/86: "Gli Stati membri possono autorizzare il ricongiungimento di altri familiari non previsti all'articolo 4, qualora essi siano a carico del rifugiato".

25 Red Cross EU office, Ecre, Distrupted flight, the realities of separated refugee families in the EU, pag. 11: "Polish authorities do not apply Article 10(2) that allows family reunification with "other" family members who are not part of the nuclear family. The reunification is therefore strictly limited to the nuclear family, i.e the spouse and underage children. There is no room for an individual assessment of a particular case when it comes to the definition of a family member. A Syrian refugee granted status in Poland wanted to be joined by his wife and children. Two daughters were already adult so they could not benefit from the family reunification procedure. The family decided that they could not leave unmarried girls alone in Syria even though they were adults. The particular situation in Syria was not taken into account".

del diritto alla vita familiare del cittadino[26] e il bilanciamento degli interessi in gioco sembra *pendere* tutto verso un interesse statale a limitare quanto più possibile non solo i numeri della migrazione irregolare ma anche quelli della migrazione legale.

Non occorre, tuttavia, particolare lungimiranza nel cogliere come la coesione di un nucleo familiare costituisca la prima forma di prevenzione sociale nei confronti di processi di devianza, di marginalizzazione e di disagio, non ultimo dei quali il disagio psichico. Eppure, dell'ovvietà di tale nesso oggi non appare affatto convinto il legislatore europeo, intento nell'ardua impresa di limitare il più possibile i flussi immigratori "altri" rispetto all'importazione regolata di mano d'opera pronta per l'uso[27]. Sembra, perciò, che una politica incentrata sull'integrazione non venga in alcun modo considerata come una possibile risposta all'attuale crisi.

In un certo senso si potrebbe anche parlare di un beneficio in termini economici per gli Stati: i familiari di beneficiari di protezione internazionale che si vedono respinta una domanda di ricongiungimento, essendo la maggior parte delle volte essi stessi rifugiati o eleggibili a protezione sussidiaria, non rinunceranno ad entrare in Europa attraverso vie illegali. Questo significa che tali persone rappresenterebbero comunque un costo per il Paese membro in termini di accoglienza.

Nel frattempo, il beneficiario di protezione internazionale che risiede legalmente sul territorio dello stesso Paese, troverà non poche difficoltà ad integrarsi nella società ospitante mentre, se avesse il supporto della famiglia ciò accadrebbe in misura minore[28].

Al contrario, incentivando il ricongiungimento per tali persone, i familiari raggiungerebbero nello Stato membro una persona che ha già parzialmente affrontato un processo d'integrazione, considerando che (in Italia) i tempi di attesa per il colloquio di fronte alla Commissione Territoriale variano tra i 6 e i

---

26 G. Sirianni, *Il diritto degli stranieri all'unità familiare,* Milano, Giuffrè, 2006.

27 P. Morozzo della Rocca, *Il diritto all'unità familiare in Europa, tra "allargamento" dei confini e "restringimento" dei diritti,* in Diritto, immigrazione e cittadinanza, 2004, n. 1, cit., pag. 63–64.

28 L'essenziale importanza di un efficace politica dei ricongiungimenti familiari ai fini dell'integrazione sociale dei già residenti è ben dimostrata nel saggio di Lynch James P. e Simon Rita J., *Saggio comparativo sul coinvolgimento criminale di immigrati e autoctoni in sette nazioni,* in Dei delitti e delle pene, 3/99, 13 ss. Si veda a questo proposito P. Morozzo della Rocca, *Il diritto all'unità familiare in Europa, tra "allargamento" dei confini e "restringimento" dei diritti,* in Diritto, immigrazione e cittadinanza, 2004, n. 1, pag. 64.

12 mesi[29] e quelli per il ricongiungimento dai 18 ai 24 mesi[30]; questo significa che, nella peggiore delle ipotesi, lo sponsor potrebbe trovarsi sul territorio del Paese ospitante da 3 anni. D'altro canto, ciò verrebbe a beneficio anche di colui al quale è stata riconosciuta la protezione internazionale, dato che il ricongiungimento costituisce la premessa essenziale per il buon esito del processo di integrazione nella vita sociale e lavorativa in Italia dello straniero, il quale può così realizzare la propria personalità, potendo contare sulla condivisione con i propri affetti. In tal senso esso deve essere considerato uno strumento necessario per permettere la vita familiare, in quanto contribuisce a creare una stabilità socio-culturale che facilita l'integrazione nello Stato, permettendo quindi di promuovere la coesione economica e sociale.

2.2 I termini per l'esame della domanda di ricongiungimento familiare: un diritto sospeso per ventiquattro mesi

Riguardo i termini per l'esame della domanda di ricongiungimento familiare, la Direttiva europea 2003/86/CE relativa al diritto al ricongiungimento familiare prevede che le autorità competenti comunichino per iscritto la loro decisione e la motivino in caso di rifiuto, *non appena possibile* e comunque entro *nove mesi* dalla data di presentazione della domanda di ricongiungimento. Solo in circostanze eccezionali il termine di nove mesi può essere prorogato. Tuttavia, in particolare con riferimento al ricongiungimento dei beneficiari di protezione internazionale, nonostante la Direttiva stabilisca tale limite di nove mesi, nella maggior parte dei Paesi Membri -compresa l'Italia- i tempi di attesa sono in media di molto superiori, variando dai 18 ai 24 mesi[31].

---

29 Si vedano le statistiche fornite da Meltingpot, (http://www.meltingpot.org/IMG/pdf/ La_procedura_di_asilo_tra_norma_e_prassi.pdf), 17.06.2016.

30 M. Benvenuti, *La protezione internazionale degli stranieri in Italia: uno studio integrato sull'applicazione dei decreti di recepimento delle direttive europee sull'accoglienza, sulle qualifiche e sulle procedure*, Napoli, Jovene, 2011, pag. 242.

31 Si veda a questo proposito quanto sostenuto dall'associazione Asilo in Europa in una rielaborazione di un intervento che l'associazione ha fatto lo scorso 23 ottobre 2014 all'interno del Laboratorio multidisciplinare sul Diritto di Asilo organizzato dal Coordinamento Non Solo Asilo presso l'Università di Torino " (…) nella maggior parte dei Paesi osservati i tempi di attesa sono in media di molto superiori ai nove mesi e variano dai 18 ai 24 mesi. Per non parlare della procedura di ricorso contro il rifiuto del rilascio del visto da parte dell'autorità consolare, che può proseguire per anni", in http://asiloineuropa.blogspot.it/2015/01/ricongiungimento-familiare-deititolari.html.

Questa estensione del tempo d'attesa per l'esame della domanda, oltre ad avere ripercussioni importanti sulla salute psicofisica del beneficiario di protezione internazionale, ha anche importanti ricadute sui familiari del migrante che si trovano nel Paese d'origine o di transito.

Per quanto riguarda il primo aspetto, la costante preoccupazione rispetto ai familiari che hanno lasciato nel loro Stato d'origine, e l'assenza di una famiglia che possa dare loro supporto nel Paese ospite, accresce la vulnerabilità di coloro ai quali è stato riconosciuto asilo, quando già sono stati esposti ad esperienze traumatiche associate alla migrazione forzata. La separazione familiare, infatti, tende ad essere associata a fragilità psicologica, che ha un impatto decisivo sulle abilità delle persone ad imparare la lingua, cercare lavoro, o semplicemente interagire con gli altri (inclusi gli ufficiali delle pubbliche amministrazioni)[32].

Con riferimento al secondo aspetto invece, le lungaggini delle ambasciate e consolati nel vagliare una domanda di ricongiungimento familiare spesso comportano un importante rischio anche per la vita/salute psico-fisica dei familiari del migrante-rifugiato: il più delle volte, la situazione in cui questi si trovano è simile – se non uguale – a quella per cui al rifugiato (o beneficiario di protezione sussidiaria) è stata riconosciuta una protezione. Molto spesso i familiari con il quale il beneficiario di protezione internazionale si vuole ricongiungere si trovano in campi profughi di Paesi confinanti a quello d'origine, dove le condizioni di vita sono assolutamente precarie o, se ancora vivono nel Paese d'origine, subiscono persecuzioni proprio in quanto familiari della persona a cui è stato riconosciuto asilo.

3 La mancanza di un dialogo tra culture

Perciò, anche con riferimento alla tutela della famiglia, l'obiettivo dell'odierna politica migratoria è centrato: consolidare nel mondo la divisione in due grandi categorie sempre più reificate; da una parte il mondo pulito, sano e visibile; dall'altra un mondo residuale, i cosiddetti 'altri', esclusi dallo sguardo, dall'attenzione e dalla coscienza della società europea[33]. Ed infatti, anche quando gli 'altri' riescono ad accedere al nostro mondo, le entrate e le uscite passano per stretti corridoi, sono filtrate da ostacoli insormontabili appositamente creati sia dal legislatore che dall'amministrazione, finalizzati a rendere quanto più vulnerabili

---

32 B. McDonald-Wilmsen, S.M. Gifford, *Refugee Resettlement, Family Separation and Australia's Humanitarian Programme. New Issues in Refugee Research*, Research Paper No. 178, Geneva: United Nations High Commissioner for Refugees, 2009.

33 Zygmunt Bauman, *Stranieri alle porte*, Roma, ed. Laterza, 2016.

i migranti e sospese le loro vite. Tutto questo a scapito della tutela del nucleo familiare di stranieri che non hanno alcuna possibilità di riunirsi con la famiglia nel loro paese d'origine.

Infine, si vuole concludere con una riflessione generale sulla mancanza, nell'odierna società e politica europea, di un "dialogo tra culture": stiamo assistendo ad un ritorno degli Stati-nazione, troppo inclinati, per loro natura, alla rivalità ed esclusione reciproca, essenzialmente riluttanti alla costruzione di una società cosmopolita, all'insegna di frontiere porose e altamente osmotiche e di una interdipendenza universale[34].

Come si è visto con riferimento specifico al diritto all'unità familiare, questo ripiegamento egoistico e poco "solidale" della politica, della società e dell'individuo altro non porta che ad una propensione a ridurre i diritti dei migranti e a mantenerli in una condizione d'insicurezza e di vulnerabilità, piuttosto che gestire il fenomeno migratorio con un approccio incentrato sui diritti[35].

Il migrante si trova così ad essere figura *svuotata di diritti* e, si noti bene, non "vuota" di diritti: la differenza la si comprende se, come già detto, si tiene in considerazione che nella normativa il rifugiato è riconosciuto come portatore di diritti (fondamentali e non) ed invece, nella prassi, le autorità preposte a dare attuazione a tali diritti, *svuotano* essenzialmente il rifugiato di tali benefici. Tale *svuotamento*, che ben si comprende analizzando l'istituto del ricongiungimento familiare, ha l'obiettivo di rendere "labirintica" la vita di tali persone e di esporle a maggiore vulnerabilità. Tale stato emotivo-psicologico, che abbiamo voluto definire come stato di *sospensione tra bisogno e desiderio*, altro non porta che ad un rallentamento o -sempre più spesso- totale fallimento del tanto agognato "processo d'integrazione".

Bibliography

Annual tripartite consultations on resettlement, Geneva, 20–21 June 2001, Background Note for the Agenda Item – *Family Reunification in the Context of Resettlement and Integration, Protecting the Family: Challenges in Implementing Policy in the Resettlement Context*

Benvenuti M., *La protezione internazionale degli stranieri in Italia: uno studio integrato sull'applicazione dei decreti di recepimento delle direttive europee sull'accoglienza, sulle qualifiche e sulle procedure*, Napoli, Jovene, 2011.

---

34 Zygmunt Bauman, *Stranieri alle porte*, Roma, ed. Laterza, 2016, pag. 56.
35 Zygmunt Bauman, *Stranieri alle porte*, Roma, ed. Laterza, 2016, pag. 79.

European Council on Refugees and Exiles (ECRE), *Submission from the European Council on Refugees and Exiles in response to the Commission's Green Paper on the right to family reunification of third-country nationals living in the European Union* (Directive 2003/86/CE).

McDonald-Wilmsen B., S.M. Gifford, *Refugee Resettlement, Family Separation and Australia's Humanitarian Programme.* New Issues in Refugee Research, Research Paper No. 178, Geneva: United Nations High Commissioner for Refugees, 2009.

Morozzo della Rocca P., *Il diritto all'unità familiare in Europa, tra "allargamento" dei confini e "restringimento" dei diritti,* in Diritto, immigrazione e cittadinanza, no. 1 2004.

Red Cross EU office, Ecre, Distrupted flight, the realities of separated refugee families in the EU

Sirianni G., *Il diritto degli stranieri all'unità familiare,* Milano, Giuffrè, 2006.

Zygmunt B., Amore Liquido, Roma, Ed. Laterza, 2003.

Zygmunt B., *Stranieri alle porte,* Roma, ed. Laterza, 2016.

Normativa, circolari e linee guida:

Circolari del Ministero dell'Interno n. 8/1995

Circolare del Ministero dell'Interno n. 2/1997

Circolare del Ministero dell'Interno, Dipartimento per le Libertà Civili e l'Immigrazione del 18.05.2015

Circolare del Ministero dell'Interno, Dipartimento per le Libertà Civili e l'Immigrazione del 17.08.2016

Decreto del Presidente della Repubblica 17 luglio 2015, n. 126 – Regolamento recante adeguamento del regolamento anagrafico della popolazione residente approvato con decreto del Presidente della Repubblica 30 maggio 1989, n. 223, alla disciplina istitutiva dell'anagrafe nazionale della popolazione residente. (15G00140) (GU Serie Generale n. 188 del 14.08.2015)

Decreto Legislativo 25 luglio 1998, n. 286, Testo unico delle disposizioni concernenti la disciplina dell'immigrazione e norme sulla condizione dello straniero, in G.U. n. 191 del 18 agosto 1998 – Suppl. Ord. n. 139, art 30 co 6

Decreto Legislativo 18 agosto 2015, n. 142, Attuazione della direttiva 2013/33/UE recante norme relative all'accoglienza dei richiedenti protezione internazionale, nonché della direttiva 2013/32/UE, recante procedure comuni ai fini del riconoscimento e della revoca dello status di protezione internazionale. (15G00158) (GU Serie Generale n. 214 del 15-09-2015)

Direttiva 2003/86/CE del Consiglio, del 22 settembre 2003 relativa al diritto al ricongiungimento familiare, in G.U. n. L 251 del 03/10/2003, pag. 0012-0018

Linee guida sul diritto alla residenza dei richiedenti e beneficiari di protezione internazionale (SPRAR, Ministero dell'Interno, UNHCR, ANUSCA, ASGI), dicembre 2014.

Stefano Piccioni

L'assistenza sessuale a persone con disabilità: materiale pedagogico e strumento di cura

Abstract: sexual assistance is an operation helping people with disabilities that is already proposed and implemented in several European nations, in the United States and Australia. In Italy, because of difficulties connected to laws and cultural taboo, this opportunity hasn't been explored yet. Despite the majority of public opinion, since several years, discuss about disabled affectivity and sexuality subject, recognizing it as a necessity, social operators working on and living with disabilities every day, were not given the chance to talk yet. With this article I wanted to investigate their knowledge level, compared to the one of sexual assistance, and their point of view on the future integration, within the world of disabilities, of o professional of this kind. From several semi-structured interviews they have been subjected to, the desire and will of an educated professional, able to manage with residential structures guests, has emerged; a professional to build with, case by case, the most suitable route to develop healthy affectivity and sexuality. On the other hand, perplexities, related to real effectiveness of this kind of intervention have emerged; intervention itself is not consider decisive for this problem and, for sure, not suitable for every kind of disability. Analysis of answers gave anyway the chance to understand that, given the operators good knowledge of this subject, there is also the awareness to be in a historical moment ready, from a social point of view too, to receive and accept a proposal like that of the sexual assistance.

1 Introduzione

L'assistenza sessuale è un intervento operato da un professionista formato a tal proposito che prevede l'accompagnamento per persone con disabilità fisica e/o mentale alla scoperta della sfera emotiva, corporea e erotica.

Le pratiche più utilizzate durante gli incontri di assistenza sessuale sono solitamente i massaggi, le carezze, giochi di scoperta del corpo e della sessualità che comprendono non solo e non necessariamente il coinvolgimento della parte genitale. Il percorso può rivolgersi anche a coppie che possono essere composte da due persone con disabilità piuttosto che due partners uno normodotato e l'altro/a con una disabilità.

La ricerca presentata in questo articolo prende le mosse dal confronto tra la situazione fuori dai confini italiani dove questa figura da anni è presente, dove i professionisti del sesso (Sex workers) sono spesso inquadrati legislativamente e dunque tutelati e riconosciuti.

In Italia, dal 2012, un movimento spontaneo capitanato da Maximiliano Ulivieri e partito da un sito web è stato capace di far emergere agli occhi pigri del dibattito pubblico l'annosa questione che riguarda il sesso e la disabilità, le zone d'ombra della legislazione e i tabù legati alla cultura nazionale. Il processo che verrà descritto in seguito nel dettaglio ha portato alla nascita di un Comitato promotore per il riconoscimento di questa nuova figura anche nel nostro paese.

All'interno di questo quadro si è deciso con questa ricerca di indagare, attraverso interviste semi-strutturate, l'opinione di undici operatori che svolgono, sulla carta, mansioni differenti all'interno di comunità residenziali che ospitano persone adulte con disabilità. Lo scopo era quello di capire, approfondendo, quale fosse lo stato dell'arte in alcune realtà strutturate, rispetto alla gestione delle esigenze affettive e sessuali degli ospiti; partendo dal racconto dell'esperienza professionale quotidiana, indagare il rapporto con l'altro (assistito e/o educando), l'atteggiamento verso gli aspetti affettivi e delle pulsioni emergenti, emerse o sopite; cercare di sondare le consapevolezze, gli umori, le prospettive costruttive o disilluse rispetto alla possibile introduzione dell'assistente sessuale nel nostro paese. La traccia di undici domande[1] ha previsto una prima parte

---

1   Traccia delle domande per l'intervista agli operatori di comunità residenziale per persone con disabilità fisica e mentale:

   1. Quante ore alla settimana lavori in comunità?
   2. Qual è la tipologia di disabilità dei vostri utenti?
   3. In cosa consiste il tuo lavoro all'interno della comunità?
   4. Quale tipologia di interventi e percorsi progettate e realizzate per i vostri utenti?
   5. Quali sono le difficoltà maggiori nella gestione e nell'assistenza dei vostri utenti?
   6. Quali sono i punti di forza principali nella gestione e nell'assistenza dei vostri utenti?
   7. Qual è il tuo atteggiamento professionale rispetto alle eventuali esigenze affettive e/o sessuali degli utenti con disabilità?
   8. Qual è la posizione della tua comunità nella gestione delle eventuali esigenze affettive e sessuali degli utenti?
   9. Conosci la figura dell'assistente sessuale? (a seguito della risposta leggere una breve descrizione della figura in questione).
  10. Credi che l'assistente sessuale possa essere una figura utile nell'ambito della disabilità in generale e perché?
  11. In quale modo si potrebbe inserire questa figura o una figura simile all'interno dei vostri percorsi terapeutico/educativo/assistenziali?

dell'intervista che introducesse la figura dell'intervistato nelle dimensioni specifiche del proprio lavoro, del suo declinarsi quotidiano nel rapporto con l'utenza e con sé stessi come professionisti. La seconda parte invece è stata strutturata in modo che vi fosse un crescendo analitico. Dagli atteggiamenti del singolo professionista, della struttura (e della sua cultura locale) rispetto alle eventuali esigenze a livello affettivo e/o sessuale degli ospiti, fino alla possibile introduzione di una figura come quella dell'assistente sessuale nei percorsi individualizzati degli stessi.

2 Il quadro internazionale dell'assistenza sessuale[2]

La definizione "assistenza sessuale" è certamente nel panorama europeo un termine piuttosto recente; con varianti linguistiche come "sexual assistance" o "assistance sexuelle" si è affermato negli ultimi anni solo all'interno di alcune nazioni europee che la contemplano e riconoscono a vari gradi. La declinazione specifica per i diversi contesti europei ha portato anche alla rinominazione della figura stessa che svolge questo tipo di assistenza: ad esempio in Svizzera il percorso prevede una figura professionale detta anche "accarezzatrice/accarezzatore". In Danimarca invece è definita come "sexual advisor", (consigliere/a sessuale). Oltre oceano, troviamo negli Stati Uniti la figura del "surrogate partner", (partner sostitutivo/a). Insomma, declinazioni sottilmente differenti per contesti e culture, riferite a morale e inquadramento legislativo altrettanto differenti; obiettivo trasversale però, a tutte le citate figure è quello del sostegno alla persona disabile nell'ambito della sessualità con percorsi individualizzati.

Diversi Paesi dell'Unione Europea come Olanda, Germania, Austria, Svizzera (parte germanica e francofona) e Danimarca riconoscono in maniera istituzionale e formale questa figura professionale anche perché tutti i servizi sessuali offerti sono già riconosciuti ufficialmente come lavoro e servizio alla comunità ed al cittadino nel caso in cui siano praticati da persone maggiorenni e consenzienti; inoltre nelle legislazioni delle nazioni citate se questi servizi sono forniti in condizioni decretate accettabili per chi li offre, per chi li riceve e per la società nel suo complesso vengono riconosciuti e sostenuti dallo Stato stesso con una serie di sgravi fiscali. In questi contesti il percorso che ha portato allo sviluppo

---

2   G.G. Geymonat: *L'assistenza sessuale in Europa: una ricerca comparata* [*Sexual Assistance in Europe: A Comparative Research*]. HP-Accaparlante, Edizioni Centro Studi Erickson: Bologna 2013, pp. 44–49.

della professione dell'assistente sessuale, a prescindere dalle differenti denominazioni definite nei diversi Stati, vede la sua genesi solitamente nell'incontro tra un'associazione di persone con disabilità ed un'associazione di persone che già fornisce questo tipo di servizi in modo non riconosciuto legislativamente, sovente associazioni di sex workers.

Le buone prassi implementate dagli stati prevedono corsi di formazione co-progettati, diplomi, formazione continuativa degli operatori, carte condivise di comportamento etico, supervisione terapeutica e prezzi concordati dalle associazioni partners.

Nella formazione dei futuri assistenti sessuali le tematiche affrontate durante i corsi propedeutici alla professione possono essere riguardanti la sfera medica, giuridica, pedagogica e assistenziale/riabilitativa. Vengono approfonditi aspetti riguardanti le varie tipologie di disabilità esistenti (fisica, mentale e sensoriale), la sessualità rispetto a concetti generali ed anche specifici nell'approccio alle persone disabili; in alcuni casi aspetti più "tecnici" come quelli legati alla legislazione ed al counseling.

In altre realtà europee invece la stessa figura od operatori simili ed equiparabili ad essa, esiste in forme non ufficialmente riconosciute e non completamente legali; Italia, Francia ed Inghilterra sono tre esempi di queste realtà. In tali situazioni l'intervento viene fornito da persone che non hanno potuto seguire corsi specializzati ed una formazione adeguata, che hanno poche protezioni e tutele legali e che possiedono e garantiscono quasi nessuna garanzia per tutte le parti coinvolte nell'assistenza. Normalmente si tratta di lavoratrici e lavoratori del sesso, munite spesso ma non necessariamente di una particolare sensibilità ed esperienza nell'approcciarsi alle persone con disabilità magari dovuta anche ad un percorso lavorativo analogo come assistenti alla persona. Troviamo dunque una massa eterogenea di massaggiatori, massaggiatrici, counselor olistici, escort, sexological bodyworker ed altre figure affini.

3 Il quadro italiano dell'assistenza sessuale

Nel corso dell'anno 2012 si è affacciato alla ribalta del mondo web, il sito www.loveability.it ideato da Maximiliano Ulivieri. Ulivieri nel suo blog personale mentre raccontava di sé e delle sue esperienze con la sessualità raccoglieva anche testimonianze di persone con differenti disabilità; la condivisione di queste storie di vita reale dal nord al sud della penisola, hanno coinvolto tutta una serie di attori (operatori sociali, genitori, semplici cittadini, esperti e parafilici), che, ognuno dal suo punto di vista, ha arricchito e alimentato il dibattito.

Con l'aiuto poi dei media che hanno implementato con servizi[3], documentari[4], film[5], articoli[6], dibattiti nei salotti anche più popolari della televisione italiana questo argomento ancora così prepotentemente tabù, si sono create le condizioni per alcuni rapidi passi verso un possibile cambiamento.

Max Ulivieri è il creatore e gestore di alcuni siti internet specifici per discutere di affettività/sessualità e disabilità come www.assistenzasessuale.it o www.lovegiver.it, del "Comitato per la promozione dell'assistenza sessuale in Italia" fondato nel gennaio del 2013 e, insieme al sessuologo e Psicoterapeuta Fabrizio Quattrini, dell'Osservatorio nazionale sull'assistenza sessuale; con lo stesso Quattrini hanno poi provveduto alla stesura dettagliata del primo corso con durata annuale per diventare assistenti sessuali(al momento autofinanziato dalle quote dei partecipanti ma non riconosciuto dallo Stato italiano). Inoltre, nell'aprile del 2014 è stato depositato un disegno di legge per l'istituzione della figura dell'assistente sessuale[7] a firma del senatore Lo Giudice e la pubblicazione del libro "Loveability: l'assistenza sessuale per le persone con disabilità" edito da Erickson nel 2014 dove Ulivieri, Quattrini e altri aderenti al Comitato raccontano l'evoluzione del percorso dello stesso e le modalità di svolgimento del corso di formazione previsto per gli aspiranti assistenti sessuali. Numerosi poi sono stati gli incontri di sensibilizzazione e formazione svolti in diverse città italiane dal 2014 ad oggi[8] che hanno portato ad un incremento dell'interesse da parte delle istituzioni politiche che nel novembre 2016 presentano alla camera dei deputati una proposta di legge per l'istituzione della figura dell'educatore per il benessere sessuale delle persone disabili[9].

Ad oggi il Comitato promotore attende che ancora l'argomento venga dibattuto nelle aule governative

---

3 https://www.iene.mediaset.it/puntate/2013/11/12/nobile-assistenza-sessuale-per-disabili_8084.shtml.
4 A. Silanus, P. Berardi: *Sesso, amore & disabilità*. Dvd, Biblioteca vivente: Bologna 2013. C. Zoratti: *the special need*. Tucker film: Germania – Italia – Austria 2013.
5 S. Bose: *Margarita, whit a straw*. Viacom 18 Motion pictures: Corea del Sud 2014; B. Lewin: *The sessions*. 20th Century Fox: USA 2012.
6 http://www.lovegiver.it/stampa-e-media/.
7 http://www.senato.it/japp/bgt/showdoc/17/DDLPRES/769165/index.html.
8 http://www.lovegiver.it/corsieconvegni/.
9 http://www.camera.it/_dati/leg17/lavori/stampati/pdf/17PDL0047910.pdf.

4 Formazione dell'assistente per la sana sessualità e il benessere psicofisico delle persone disabili in Italia

Il contesto italiano ha richiesto una revisione della figura come presentata negli stati dove la normativa sui "sex workers" è già molto chiara. In Italia il rischio è che si possa strumentalizzare la posizione rispetto all'argomento prostituzione, mutuandola alla nuova figura professionale definita dalla proposta di legge come *"assistente per la sana sessualità e il benessere psicofisico delle persone con disabilità o assistente sessuale"*[10]. I promotori hanno voluto mostrare ai detrattori e scettici sull'argomento, come la figura pensata e tradotta sia assolutamente unica nel suo genere, ben distante anche dai riferimenti esteri dove gli omologhi sono sovente inquadrati, in materia di lavoro, alla stregua degli altri professionisti della prostituzione. Infatti, il/la professionista per il contesto italiano sarà, nell'ipotesi progettuale, un/a operatore/ice che a seguito di un percorso di formazione di tipo psicologico, sessuologico e medico, dovrà essere in grado di aiutare le persone con disabilità fisico-motoria e/o psichico/cognitiva a vivere un'esperienza erotica, sensuale o sessuale e a indirizzare al meglio le proprie energie interne spesso scaricate in modo disfunzionale in sentimenti di rabbia e aggressività.

L'aspirante assistente dovrà partecipare a un percorso formativo di circa 200 ore distribuite nell'arco di 12 mesi con incontri a cadenza mensile[11]. Per accedere a questo corso sarà necessaria una preventiva e molto accurata selezione tra i candidati[12]. Soltanto i candidati ritenuti idonei da questa iniziale e rigorosa selezione potranno avere accesso al corso di formazione strutturato sia a livello teorico che pratico.

Il colloquio clinico vero e proprio è stato definito lo strumento principe del protocollo sperimentale, che si vorrebbe trasformare in linea guida per il Ministero della salute e per gli interventi legislativi delle regioni che avrebbero comunque, ampio margine di autonomia sulla definizione e la modalità di riconoscimento di tale figura professionale.

Soltanto i candidati ritenuti idonei da questa iniziale e rigorosa selezione potranno avere accesso al corso di formazione strutturato sia a livello teorico che pratico.

---

10 http://www.senato.it/japp/bgt/showdoc/17/DDLPRES/769165/index.html.

11 M. Ulivieri: *Loveability. L'assistenza sessuale per le persone con disabilità*. Erickson: Trento 2014, pp. 79–81.

12 M. Ulivieri: *Loveability. L'assistenza sessuale per le persone con disabilità*. Erickson: Trento 2014, pp. 75–79.

5 Prospettive degli operatori della residenzialità

Gli operatori della residenzialità protetta sono coloro che da sempre insieme alle famiglie delle persone disabili hanno affrontato, o a volte ignorato, le esigenze potenti dei loro utenti; spesso hanno visto e lottato con la traduzione di queste esigenze in energia incanalata in maniera disfunzionale, aggressiva, depressoide, compulsiva, da sedare o comunque da tenere sotto controllo. Molte volte hanno aggirato le norme trovando soluzioni "creative". Dalle loro interviste emerge una situazione faticosa, innanzitutto per l'onere di una professione usurante, per la consapevolezza e allo stesso tempo l'impotenza, della difficoltà nell'affrontare e gestire la tematica sessualità e disabilità. Questo dovuto anche al fatto che hanno descritto un mestiere che è cambiato nel tempo, sempre più inevitabilmente flessibile e che ha richiesto competenze trasversali, oscillante tra la cura assistenziale in senso stretto e l'intervento educativo e pedagogico; competenze che hanno contemporaneamente arricchito, confuso ed affaticato, promuovendo una nuova figura a cavallo tra l'educazione e l'assistenza che venalmente risponda alla mancanza di risorse economiche:

"…spesso l'educatore non c'è in turno banalmente, detto questo e quindi ti tocca al di là della figura che hai di prendere delle decisioni o di relazionarsi in un modo, come dire, pedagogico, educativo con l'utente in modo o da contenerlo o da calmarlo o di spiegargli delle situazioni, di farlo rientrare in un momento loro che hanno spesso di forte stress o ansia importante o di disagio, di malessere…".

"…io come educatrice mi occupo prevalentemente di organizzare quelle che sono le giornate a livello educativo, in realtà facciamo un po' di tutto, nel senso che, essendo la casa dove vivono i ragazzi, ci occupiamo del cucinare, lavare, aiutarli a vestirsi e a fare l'igiene…".

Le loro risposte hanno mostrato una serie di ostacoli burocratici e morali, formali e informali, personali e culturali alla presa in carico totale delle richieste degli ospiti tra i quali la troppa sanitarizzazione, il bisogno di proceduralizzare tutto per lasciare traccia scritta, la mancanza di formazione specifica su alcuni temi/ ambiti, le resistenze culturali delle famiglie o degli amministratori di sostegno.

Nello stesso tempo è emersa la presenza di una serie di piccoli interventi, di una microprogettualità, di brevi percorsi inerenti il tema, efficaci ma non sufficienti: dal riconoscimento delle proprie emozioni e sensazioni corporee ad altrettanto brevi training all'autoerotismo e ai contesti più adeguati nei quali metterlo in atto. Dalle loro risposte si è percepita ancora tanta professionalità al servizio delle fasce più deboli, una notevole dose di competenza, esperienza che, messa nelle condizioni ottimali per operare, ha attestato una sollecita capacità di analisi dei contesti e dei bisogni, la motivazione, a volte un pò sopita per l'usura del contesto lavorativo, a sperimentare e sperimentarsi in una presa in carico dei soggetti integrata ed organica.

A fronte di una tale condizione di contesto lavorativo si è evinto dalle risposte della maggioranza degli intervistati una parziale conoscenza della figura dell'assistente sessuale nella formula esistente all'estero e poca o nulla conoscenza invece del percorso di sensibilizzazione e promozione che è stato svolto in Italia dal Comitato promotore per l'assistenza sessuale:

> "...non so come operino, nel senso che non so se si tratta di un accompagnare la persona o anche a partecipare a a a un atto sessuale vissuto o fatto in un modo o nell'altro, questo non lo so, magari ci sono diverse modalità di lavorare in questo senso.".

Non tutti i soggetti intervistati, nonostante nella loro pratica quotidiana si siano trovati più volte spaesati e senza strumenti nella gestione della sfera affettiva e sessuale di alcuni utenti, si sono dimostrati concordi sull'efficacia dell'intervento di questa nuova figura professionale. Una minoranza perplessa non tanto sulle capacità del nuovo professionista quanto sull'utilità dell'intervento stesso per alcune tipologie di disabilità (soprattutto mentale grave, incapace forse di gestire le conseguenze emotive che l'intervento potrebbe provocare). A questa preoccupazione si assommi poi il sovraccarico di lavoro per gli operatori che la gestione di queste eventuali conseguenze potrebbe comportare:

> "...allora, questa è una cosa molto complicata, indubbiamente, ovvio che l'aspetto sessuale per una persona è importantissimo, io penso cheee, bisogna conoscere, intanto bisogna essere formati benissimo come assistente sessuale e bisogna conoscere molto bene la persona...non so, ho alcune perplessità, nel senso che, un utente, arrivato a 50 anni senza esperienze, non so quanto, perché poi alla fine cosa cerchiamo, noi cerchiamo il bene della persona, il bene di una persona non è detto che sia fargli provare un rapporto sessuale a 50 anni, perché, perché potrebbe farlo entrare in problematiche che fino a quel momento non ha mai vissuto...".

La maggior parte invece degli interpellati ha considerato con favore l'inserimento di questa nuova figura professionale all'interno del mondo della disabilità per una serie di motivi: in primis una figura finalmente formata sul tema, focalizzata nell'ambito specifico che permetta di liberare risorse professionali su altri interventi supplendo alla mancanza di strumenti specifici, alle strategie e soluzioni alternative spesso improvvisate. In secondo luogo, per canalizzare in maniera più efficacie tutte quelle energie e pulsioni sovente espresse con azioni disfunzionali come rabbia, aggressività o depressione. Un terzo aspetto potrebbe essere in prospettiva la riduzione per alcuni utenti dell'assunzione di psicofarmaci utilizzati spesso per sedare l'energia mal canalizzata:

> "...ad alcuni servirebbe tantissimo, cioè proprio, risolverebbe, non dico il 50 ma il 30 per cento di quello che magari fanno i farmaci piuttosto che, potrebbe dare dei benefici tecnici, oggettivi, rilevanti, secondo me, soprattutto su chi, sì magari ha un ritardo mentale di un

certo tipo ma anche una carica sessuale alle stelle che lo porta poi a fare delle cose che, ovviamente, deve gestire il suo istinto...".

Gli operatori sono risultati unanimi riguardo al fatto che, se fosse introdotta la figura dell'assistente sessuale come descritta dal Comitato promotore[13], dovrebbe divenire parte integrante dell'equipe di lavoro e quindi corresponsabile di una presa in carico dell'utente globale e condivisa a partire dal progetto individualizzato. Altrettanto condivisa la posizione che la figura delineata possa da un lato essere una risorsa all'interno delle strutture dall'altro che non sia adeguata per tutte le tipologie di disabilità e in determinati momenti dei percorsi di vita.

6 Conclusioni

La ricerca proposta in questo articolo è iniziata descrivendo i contesti stranieri nei quali la figura dell'assistente sessuale, in varie forme, è già presente da anni. Culture differenti da quella italiana che sono state in grado di alimentare una discussione interna tra attori sociali, istituzioni politiche e opinione pubblica; paesi che hanno saputo rispondere in maniera rapida ed efficace ad un diritto universale, ad un'esigenza, un desiderio, a volte un bisogno che, talmente urgente, non può e non deve rimanere sospeso.

La capacità di dialogare tra culture differenti, l'opportunità di condividere buone prassi e mutuare esempi virtuosi di gestione delle criticità sono stati in buona parte i presupposti che hanno spinto il Comitato promotore per l'assistenza sessuale in Italia a perorare la causa che ha coinvolto la società civile a più livelli: dalla cittadinanza, agli addetti ai lavori fino alle istituzioni politiche. Un dialogo che, in un moto centripeto, è andato dalle culture legislative dei paesi che riconoscono i sex workers verso il più rigido contesto italiano, generando la possibilità di una rimodulazione della proposta professionale; una figura, quella descritta nel decreto di legge presentato in Senato, adattata per contesti pronti ad includerla e per la quale è stato costruito un percorso formativo accurato e professionalizzante. Molti degli operatori intervistati nelle strutture residenziali per persone con disabilità sono stati concordi con la necessità di trovare in breve tempo una soluzione per la gestione degli aspetti affettivo-sessuali dell'utenza; la proposta presentata all'equipes di lavoro di una figura competente, formata, collaborante nella presa in carico globale della persona e con specifici vincoli d'intervento etico-professionali è stata accolta con parere molto positivo.

---

13 M. Ulivieri: *Loveability. L'assistenza sessuale per le persone con disabilità.* Erickson: Trento 2014, pp. 70–71.

Questa ricerca mostra come lo spazio per introdurre la figura dell'assistente sessuale sia stato creato. Lo si è evinto dalla storia dell'assistenza sessuale nel nostro paese, dal dibattito pubblico che l'ha resa visibile, da un primo timido riconoscimento formale delle istituzioni, ma soprattutto dalle parole dei protagonisti, persone con disabilità sia fisica che mentale, un numero sempre maggiore di famiglie e di operatori del settore ai quali è stato negato un diritto fondamentale lasciandoli sospesi tra il bisogno e il desiderio. La sfera di tabù che ha circondato l'argomento ha impedito che il dialogo tra le differenti culture si avviasse e portasse al confronto, all'evoluzione e al processo di negoziazione sociale che, a partire dal 2012 attraverso il sito di Max Ulivieri, ha invece avuto inizio.

L'assistente sessuale è una figura assolutamente non risolutiva di un sistema culturale più ampio che comprende la discriminazione e il miraggio di canoni estetici estremamente selettivi e modalità di approccio all'Altro sempre più ricche di pregiudizi e indifferenza. Nessuna presunzione salvifica nella proposta di questa nuova professione; quello che è emerso da questa ricerca è il desiderio di poter fornire una scelta, un'alternativa, un'opportunità di essere liberi di partecipare.

Bibliografia

Basaglia, Franco/Ongaro Basaglia, Franca/Pirella, Agostino/Taverna, Salvatore: *La nave che affonda*. Cortina: Milano 2008.

Bose, Shonali: *Margarita, whit a straw*. Viacom 18 Motion pictures: Corea del Sud 2014.

Caprara, GianVittorio/Barbaranelli, Claudio/Pastorelli, Concetta/Perugini, Marco: *Indicatori della condotta aggressiva. Irritabilità e ruminazione/ dissipazione: manuale*. Organizzazioni speciali: Firenze 1991.

Caprara, GianVittorio/Barbaranelli, Claudio/Pastorelli, Concetta/Perugini, Marco: *Scala per la misurazione della fragilità emotiva: manuale*. Organizzazioni speciali: Firenze 1991.

Cohen Green, Cheryl/Garano, Lorna: *An intimate life. Sex, love and my journey as a surrogate partner*. Soft skull press: New York 2012.

De Vries, Nina: *Close encounters of the lovely kind*, retrieved 14.7.2017 from http://ninadevries.com/english/index.html.

Dufour, Pierre: *L'expérience handie. Handicap et virilité*. Presses universitaires de Grenoble: Grenoble 2013.

Gendarme, Remi: *Je n'accepterais aucune assistante sexuelle si lui faire l'amour ne la fait pas elle- meme trembler de plaisir*. Editions FLBLB: Poitiers 2014.

Geymonat, Giulia Garofalo: *L'assistenza sessuale in Europa: una ricerca comparata.* HP-Accaparlante, Edizioni Centro Studi Erickson: Bologna 2013.

International Professional Surrogates Association: *What is Surrogate Partner Therapy?*, retrieved 14.7.2017 from http://www.surrogatetherapy.org/what-is-surrogate-partner-therapy/.

Lewin, Ben: *The sessions.* 20th Century Fox: USA 2012.

Liccardo, Tiziana/Ricciardi, Alessandra/DeConciliis, Serafino/Valerio, Paolo: *Affettività, relazioni e sessualità nella persona con disabilità tra barriere familiari e opportunità istituzionali.* Federiciana editrice universitaria: Napoli 2015.

Lo Giudice, Sergio: *Atto Senato n. 1442*, retrieved 14.7.2017 from http://www.senato.it/leg/17/BGT/Schede/Ddliter/44296.htm.

Masters, William/Johnson, Virginia: *Human sexual inadequacy.* Bantam books: Toronto-New York 1970.

Mehrabian, Albert: *Balanced emotional empathy scale: manuale.* Adattamento italiano a cura di Meneghini, Anna Maria/Sartori, Riccardo/Cunico, Laura. Organizzazioni speciali: Firenze 1996.

Nobile, Sabrina: *Assistenza sessuale per disabili*, retrieved 10.7.2017 from http://www.befan.it/le-iene-nobile-assistenza-sessuale-per-disabili-puntata-del-12-novembre.

Nuss, Marcel: *Handicaps et sexualités.* Dunod: Paris 2008.

Nuss, Marcel: *Je veux faire l'amour. Handicap, sexualité, liberté.* Editions autrement: Paris 2012.

ONU: *Convenzione nazionale sui diritti delle persone con disabilità.* ONU: Ginevra 2006.

Pellizzi, Marta: *La genesi*, retrieved 10.7.2017 from http://www.loveability.it/la-genesi/.

Poli, Simona: *Sesso e disabili pronti a lottare per abbattere l'ultimo tabù*, retrieved 10.7.2017 from http://ricerca.repubblica.it/repubblica/archivio/repubblica/2015/01/23/sesso-e-disabili-pronti-a-lottare-per-abbattere-lultimo-tabuFirenze05.html.

Quattrini, Fabrizio: *Il progetto*, retrieved 10.7.2017 from http://www.lovegiver.it/il-progetto/

Redattore Sociale: *Assistenza sessuale ai disabili, il governatore della Toscana firma la risoluzione*, retrieved 10.7.2017 from http://www.redattoresociale.it/Notiziario/Articolo/478698/Assistenza-sessuale-ai-disabili-il-governatore-della-Toscana-firma-la-risoluzione.html.

Saja, Francesco: *Sentenza n. 561 anno 1987*, retrieved 14.7.2017 from http://www.giurcost.org/decisioni/1987/0561s-87.html.

Sclavi, Marianella: *Arte di ascoltare e mondi possibili. Come si esce dalle cornici di cui siamo parte*. Bruno Mondadori: Milano 2003.

Silanus, Adriano/Berardi, Priscilla: *Sesso, amore & disabilità*. Dvd, Biblioteca vivente: Bologna 2013.

Summermatter, Stefania: *Oltre l'handicap, il diritto alla sessualità*, retrieved 14.7.2017 from http://www.swissinfo.ch/ita/oltre-l-handicap—il-diritto-alla-sessualit%C3%A0/7481886.

Ulivieri, Maximiliano: *LoveAbility – L'assistenza sessuale per le persone con disabilità*, retrieved 15.7.2017 from http://www.assistenzasessuale.it/libro-loveability-lassistenza-sessuale-per-disabilita/.

Ulivieri, Maximiliano: *Loveability: l'assistenza sessuale per le persone con disabilità*. Erickson: Trento 2014.

Vatré, Françoiss/Diserens, Catherine Agathe: *Assistance sexuelle et handicap. Au désir des corps, réponses sensuelles et sexuelles avec créativité*. Chronique sociale: Lyon 2012.

Veglia, Fabio: *Handicap e sessualità: il silenzio, la voce, la carezza*. Franco Angeli: Milano 2000.

Wurth, Giorgia: *L'accarezzatrice*. Mondadori: Milano 2014.

Zoratti, Carlo: *the special need*. Tucker film: Germania- Italia- Austria 2013.

IV   Dialogue of languages and dialogue through the language

Mihaela Mihova und Valerio Fidenzi

Introduction

The dialogue of cultures goes hand in hand both with the dialogue of languages, and with the dialogue through the language. The former occurs when the encounter of cultures ends up triggering a number of linguistic phenomena like second language acquisition. The latter occurs when language becomes the tool through which the image of a target culture is shaped and presented to the eyes of the source culture.

Overall, the following two chapters present and discuss situations in which language plays a key role in the dialogue between cultures. This, for instance, happens when second languages are acquired in Sweden (see Mihova), and the choice of the second language itself in a multilingual context, thus the choice between German, Spanish and other "competing" languages, is revealing of both the speaker's own identity and of the role played by the foreign language in the speaker's culture. But language is also one of the most important means through which foreign cultures are described to – and therefore understood by – the source culture. Journalistic writing, for instance, shapes the perception of the foreign culture and might consequently end up giving birth to stereotypes (see Fidenzi). When the foreign culture is particularly far away and contacts reduced to the minimum, as is the case for the small island of Tristan da Cunha, the language used in the news pieces is likely to be the only means of contact between the target culture, namely the island, and the source culture, namely Britain, thus the only filter between the two (especially when taking into account historical news reporting), and this has relevant consequences in the shaping of the socio-political image of the target culture.

In her chapter, Mihaela Mihova focuses on German and its role in Sweden nowadays. Even if Sweden has only one official language, there are plenty of languages in dialogue in the Swedish society: Swedish but also minority languages, the languages of multilingual people as well as foreign languages learned in school and other contexts. As these languages meet each other in different constellations, they influence each other and the speakers are used to switching languages depending on the context. Multilingualism and different language variations have become a part of the identity of people living in Sweden. For a long time, German has played a key role both in the society and in the Swedish educational system. It is one of the most popular foreign languages next to Spanish and French. The objective of Mihova's chapter is to illustrate the motives of Swedish high school students for choosing German as a foreign language as well as their attitudes towards German and the German-speaking countries. The chapter is based on an empirical research, composed of qualitative interviews in Sweden with pupils from five high schools in Stockholm. It could be stated that the main motives for learning German have to do with family and the similarity between Swedish and German. Further, the possibility for using German for travelling, studying and working also plays a significant role. German is in "competition" with other foreign languages in the curriculum like Spanish, which presently enjoys increasing popularity among pupils in Sweden. The wide variety of foreign languages offered encourages the pupils to make a decision concerning their own motives, which, as the study shows, often correspond with individual interests and are part of the pupil's identity.

Valerio Fidenzi's chapter focuses on selected instances of dialogue between the United Kingdom and Tristan da Cunha, a British overseas territory in the South Atlantic Ocean consisting in a small island of volcanic origin that can rightfully be considered the remotest inhabited place in the world. The relevant instances of dialogue analysed in the chapter are pieces of news published in Britain between 1816, the year of colonisation of the island, and 1949, the end of the non-industrialised part of the history of Tristan da Cunha. The aim is to bring to the fore the picture of Tristan emerging from the news pieces, thus to understand what socio-political image of Tristan da Cunha did British news published in the above-mentioned period contribute to shaping. This is of particular interest especially considering the fact that most of the early settlers of the island were British compatriots until few decades before the news pieces were written. To this aim, Fidenzi examines both manually and with the software tool *Sketch Engine* a corpus of 163 articles published by a number of newspapers from cities such as Plymouth, Portsmouth, London, Sheffield, Manchester, Belfast, Edinburgh and Dundee. Overall, the analysis of those articles published in the 19th century reveals both the generally little visibility given by the British press to the island, and a kind of discourse anchored to a rhetoric of isolation that often fails to bring the focus on the urgent needs that the community was facing during the early decades of colonisation. At the turn of the century, diverging tendencies are highlighted. On the one hand, the boost in the publication of articles pertaining to Tristan between 1900 and 1909 seems to put an end to the solitude of the island, but the outbreak of two world conflicts ends up overshadowing, once again, the island, and putting it face-to-face with its ever-lasting problem of visibility and newsworthiness. On the other hand, the Crown's assumption of responsibility and the emergence of peculiar island customs start triggering the press' interest, and this results in the publication of more detailed and realistic pieces of news, in which the hardships of colonising an isolated island are not given for granted anymore.

As shown in the two chapters, the dialogue of languages can have many different shapes, purposes and consequences, depending on time, context and medium. The chief message of Mihova's chapter is that language is a bridge between cultures, enabling the dialogue as a social practice between individuals. In turn, Fidenzi's work highlights how this dialogue, even when unequal in itself and between unequal cultures, can raise awareness on specific issues and eventually improve the living conditions of a community.

Mihaela Mihova

Motivationen? Den är på toppen! Motive schwedischer Schüler_innen für die Wahl der deutschen Sprache Einstellungen zur deutschen Sprache und zum amtlich deutschsprachigen Raum

Abstract: This chapter focuses on a research about German in Sweden. It's objective was to illustrate the motives of Swedish high school students for choosing German as a foreign language as well as to elucidate their attitudes towards German and the German-speaking countries. The study was based on an empirical research, composed of qualitative interviews in Sweden, divided into a pre-study with German teachers and a main study with pupils studying German. The following chapter has the goal to present both the theoretical background and the main results of the study. Besides, it shall illustrate the "dialogue of languages" (especially Swedish and German) among the investigated group, a dialogue which could be seen as a part of the pupil's language identity.

1 Einleitung

Schon lange spielt die deutsche Sprache sowohl in der schwedischen Gesellschaft als auch in der schwedischen Schule eine wichtige Rolle. Bedingt durch bis in die Hansezeit zurückreichende Beziehungen zwischen dem deutschen und dem schwedischen Sprachraum hat Deutsch deutliche Spuren in der schwedischen Sprache hinterlassen.[1] Bis Anfang des 20. Jahrhunderts war Deutsch zudem die in Schweden meist verbreitete Fremdsprache. Mittlerweile hat, angesichts einer zunehmenden Globalisierung, Englisch diese Position eingenommen. Zugleich gewinnt auch Spanisch auf Kosten des Deutschen an Bedeutung. Parallel dazu gibt es aber ökonomische Entwicklungen, die erneut die Bedeutung des Deutschen in der schwedischen Gesellschaft wachsen lassen: Der Bedarf an

---

1   So wurden beispielsweise im Schwedischen de Präfixe „be-" oder „an-" Deutschem übernommen; vgl. Wessén, Elias: *Om det tyska inflytandet på svenskt språk under medeltiden.* 3. Auflage. Kungl. Boktryckeriet: Stockholm 1970.

Arbeitskräften mit Deutschkenntnissen in verschiedenen Sektoren wie Tourismus, Wirtschaft, Wissenschaft oder Technik ist steigend[2].

Vor diesem Hintergrund setzt sich der vorliegende Beitrag mit der Stellung
der deutschen Sprache unter jungen Deutschlernenden in Schweden auseinander. Das zentrale Anliegen ist, den Motiven schwedischer Schüler_innen am
Gymnasium, d.h. im Alter zwischen 16 und 18 Jahren, bei der Wahl des Deutschen als Fremdsprache nachzugehen sowie deren Einstellungen zur deutschen
Sprache und zum amtlich deutschsprachigen Raum zu untersuchen. Die Schü-
ler_innen, die im Mittelpunkt des vorliegenden Beitrags stehen, haben bereits
einige Jahre Sprachlernerfahrungen hinter sich und können so einerseits darüber berichten, warum sie sich für Deutsch entschieden haben, andererseits
können sie aber auch schon erste Beurteilungen zu ihrer Entscheidung für die
deutsche Sprache abgeben.

2 Theoretischer Hintergrund: Motive, Einstellungen und Motivation beim Fremdsprachenlernen

2.1 Motive und Einstellungen

In der Spracherwerbsforschung wird unter einem Motiv meist die Bereitschaft
verstanden, bestimmte Ziele anzustreben und bestimmte Handlungen auszufüh-
ren. Menschliche Handlungen werden durch Motive ausgelöst, aufrechterhalten
oder beendet[3]. Motive zum Erlernen einer Fremdsprache werden als Bewegg-
gründe angesehen, welche in der Persönlichkeit und Biographie der Lernenden,
aber auch in der Lernumgebung, in den Einstellungen und Orientierungen zur
Zielsprache und der damit verbundenen Kultur angesiedelt sind[4].

In eine etwas andere Richtung verweist der Begriff der Einstellung. Während
Motive die Beweggründe umfassen, die zum Erlernen einer Fremdsprache füh-
ren, beschreiben Einstellungen die Menge der Kategorien, die ein Individuum
zur subjektiven Bewertung sozialer Gegenstände (Objekte, Personen, Werte,

---

2 Petersson, Kenny: *Tyska förlorar mark i Europa. Statistiska centralbyrån*. Zuletzt gelesen
   am 06.01.2016 von http://www.scb.se/sv_/Hitta-statistik/Artiklar/Tyska-spraket-for-
   lorar-mark-i-Europa/.

3 Kleppin, Karin: Der Faktor Motivation in der individuellen Sprachlernberatung.
   In: Küppers, Almut/Quetz, Jürgen (Hrsg.): *Motivation Revisited. Festschrift für Gert
   Solmecke*. Lit Verlag: Berlin 2006 S. 57–68, S. 58.

4 Riemer, Claudia: Motivation. In: Barkowski, Hans/Krumm, Hans-Jürgen (Hrsg.): *Fachlexikon Deutsch als Fremd- und Zweitsprache*. A. Franke Verlag: Tübingen/Basel 2010,
   S. 219–220, hier S. 219.

Gruppen, Ideen) verwendet[5]. Gemäß Städtler (1998) bestehen Einstellungen aus kognitiven, affektiven und handlungsintentionalen Komponenten. Die kognitive Komponente bezieht sich auf verschiedene Wissenselemente, beispielsweise Überzeugungen. Die affektive oder bewertende Komponente ist im Bereich der Gefühle angesiedelt, während die handlungsintentionale Komponente als Ausdruck einer Verhaltensabsicht gilt[6].

Motive und Einstellungen gelten als Grundlage von Motivation, die individuelles Verhalten bewegt oder verursacht[7].

2.2 Motivation

Motivation ist für zielgerichtetes menschliches Handeln zuständig[8]. Gardner (1985) definiert Motivation wie folgt:

> Motivation to learn a second language is seen as referring to the extent to which the individual works or strives to learn the language because of a desire to do so and the satisfaction experienced in this activity[9].

Daraus ergibt sich, dass motivierte Fremdsprachenlerner_innen Freude am Lernen haben und bereit sind, Eigeninitiative zu ergreifen. Motivation wird in der Spracherwerbsforschung als ein durch Emotionen geprägtes Lernmerkmal beschrieben, welches einen wesentlichen Einfluss auf den Erfolg und die Schnelligkeit des Erlernens einer Sprache ausübt[10].

Dass eine Person motiviert ist, ist laut Gardner anhand von zwei Beobachtungskategorien erkennbar: Ein Individuum übt eine zielgerichtete Aktivität aus und dies ist mit einem Arbeitsaufwand verbunden. Weiters hebt er hervor, dass bei motivierten Personen nicht nur der Wunsch nach dem Erreichen des Ziels vorhanden ist, sondern auch eine positive Einstellung gegenüber der Handlung selbst[11]. Moti-

5   Sherif, Carolyn/Sherif, Muzafer (1969): *Social Psychology*. Harper & Row: New York 1969 S. 336 f.
6   Städtler, Thomas: *Lexikon der Psychologie*. Wörterbuch. Handbuch. Studienbuch. Kröner: Stuttgart 1998, S. 222.
7   Vgl. Riemer 2010, S. 219.
8   Dörnyei, Zoltán: *Motivational Strategies in the Language Classroom*. University Press: Cambridge 2001, S. 117
9   Gardner, Robert: *Social Psychology and Second Language Learning. The Role of Attitudes and Motivation*. Edward Arnold: London 1985 S. 10.
10 Vgl. Riemer 2010, S. 219.
11 Vgl. Gardner 1985, S. 50.

vation kann allerdings unterschiedlich stark ausgeprägt sein und Schwankungen unterliegen[12].

Die Motivation zum Erlernen einer Fremdsprache setzt sich aus unterschiedlichen, sich überlappenden, komplementären und interdependenten Komponenten zusammen, welche in der Persönlichkeit der Lernenden, in deren Einstellungen und Orientierungen gegenüber der zu erlernenden Fremdsprache (und der Zielkultur) sowie in der Lernumgebung und im soziokulturellen Milieu wurzeln[13].

3 Bisherige Forschungsergebnisse

3.1 Länderübergreifende Studie: Motive, Deutsch zu lernen

Riemer (2012) untersuchte die Motive für das Erlernen von Deutsch als Fremdsprache in insgesamt 19 Ländern. Die zentrale Datengrundlage dafür stellte je eine länderspezifische Sammlung von schriftlichen Sprachlernbiographien, semi-strukturierten Lerner_innen- und Expert_inneninterviews, Dokumentenanalysen und Unterrichtsbeobachtungen dar. Untersucht wurden sowohl Länder in geographischer Nähe als auch Länder in geographischer Entfernung zum amtlich deutschsprachigen Raum. Das Sampling bestand vorwiegend aus Germanistikstudierenden, in einigen Ländern wurden auch Schüler_innen befragt[14].

Insgesamt konnte Riemer überwiegend positive Einstellungen zur Fremdsprache Deutsch feststellen. Deutsch wurde als eine wichtige Sprache in der EU betrachtet, die zwar als schwer erlernbar und herausfordernd wahrgenommen, aber auch als schön klingend und anziehend beurteilt wurde. Deutschkenntnissen wurde in Riemers Studie teils ein besonderer Status zugeschrieben: Da nicht alle Deutsch können, genießt Deutsch den Status des Besonderen. Als Motive für das Erlernen der deutschen Sprache hoben die befragten Studierenden und Schüler_innen den instrumentellen Nutzen des Deutschen hervor. Dahinter stand die Annahme, dass Deutschkenntnisse für den künftigen Beruf von Nutzen sein werden (beispielsweise in sprachbezogenen Berufen, wie Lehrer_in,

---

12 Vgl. Riemer 2010, S. 219.
13 Riemer, Claudia: Motivation in der empirischen Fremdsprachenforschung. In: Küppers, Almut/Quetz, Jürgen (Hrsg.): *Motivation Revisited. Festschrift für Gert Solmecke.* Lit Verlag: Berlin 2006, S. 35–48, S. 36.
14 Riemer, Claudia: „Warum Deutsch (noch) gelernt wird – Motivationsforschung und Deutsch als Fremdsprache". In: Barkowski, Hans et al. (Hrsg.): *Deutsch bewegt. Entwicklungen in der Auslandsgermanistik und Deutsch als Fremd- und Zweitsprache.* Baltmannsweiler: Schneider 2012, S. 330 f.

Dolmetscher_in, Übersetzer_in oder auch in anderen Bereichen, wie im Tourismus). Als weiteres Motiv für das Deutschlernen wurde in Riemers Forschungsarbeit auch das Interesse an der Kultur der amtlich deutschsprachigen Länder und die Lust, diese Länder zu bereisen und Kontakte zu knüpfen, genannt. Hinzu kamen Motive, die im Unterrichtskontext selbst zu verorten sind. Einerseits wurden positive Erfahrungen und Erfolgserlebnisse im Deutschunterricht seitens der Lernenden gemacht, andererseits wurde als Grund für die Wahl von Deutsch als Fremdsprache angeführt, dass keine oder nur wenig attraktive Alternativen angeboten wurden. Eine weitere wesentliche Rolle schienen auch Eltern, Familienmitglieder und Freunde zu spielen. Wie Riemers Länderstudien zeigen, beeinflussten diese die Entscheidung, Deutsch zu lernen, wesentlich[15].

3.2 Schwedenbezogene Studien: Gründe gegen Deutsch

In Schweden wurden diverse Studien zur Fremdsprachenwahl im Schulbereich durchgeführt. Was die Gründe für die Abwahl des Deutschen betrifft, ist Edlerts und Bergseths (2003) Untersuchung zu Einstellungen zum Sprachunterricht nennenswert. Die Autor_innen suchten nach Gründen, warum eine bestimmte Sprache nicht gewählt wurde. Als Gründe gegen das Deutsche gaben die befragten Schüler_innen an, dass die Sprache „hässlich" sei und dass sie „schlecht" und „einförmig" klinge. Außerdem habe man kein Interesse daran, nach Deutschland zu fahren. Die deutsche Grammatik gelte als schwer und es könne insgesamt als „lächerlich" angesehen werden, Deutsch zu lernen[16]. Weitere Gründe gegen Deutsch hängen damit zusammen, dass die Eltern, sofern sie die Sprache gelernt haben, nicht wirklich davon profitieren konnten[17].

In den letzten Jahren durchgeführte Abschlussarbeiten bestätigen diese Ergebnisse: Es zeigt sich, dass die deutsche Sprache pauschal betrachtet ein schlechtes Ansehen unter schwedischen Schüler_innen genießt und als schwierig und hässlich aufgefasst wird[18]. In Interviews befragte Schüler_innen geben an, dass Deutsch ihrem Empfinden nach nicht schön klinge und eine schwer erlernbare

---

15 Vgl. Riemer 2012, S. 333–336.
16 Edlert, Maria/ Bergseth, Elsa: *Attitydundersökning om språkstudier i grundskola och gymnasieskola, Resultat av en kvalitativ undersökning.* Andreas Lund & Co AB, Myndigheten för skolutveckling: Stockholm 2003, S. 21.
17 Vgl. Edlert/Bergseth 2003, S. 36.
18 Tendzeric, Biljana/Töttrup, Sara: *Tyska med elevers ögon. En studie om elevers attityd till ämnet tyska och dess undervisning.* 2008 Zuletzt gelesen am 21.01.2016 von http://www.diva-portal.org/smash/get/diva2:238505/FULLTEXT01.pdf 2008.

Sprache sei. Häufig genannte Assoziationen zum Deutschen sind: Krieg, Nazis, Hitler, eine heftige und strenge Aussprache, schwierige Grammatik.[19].

4 Methodik und Design der Studie

„Motive und Einstellungen" sind abstrakte, nicht objektiv messbare Phänomene. Als solche lassen sie sich am besten mittels eines möglichst offenen Interviewverfahrens ermitteln[20], welches die Möglichkeit für die interviewten Personen eröffnet, „ihre Subjektivität zu entfalten und die gestellten Fragen möglichst frei und ungehindert zu beantworten"[21].

Für die vorliegende Studie wurden im Großraum Stockholm einerseits zwei Expertinneninterviews mit zwei Deutschlehrkräften[22], andererseits zwölf Interviews mit Schüler_innen im Alter von 16 bis 18 Jahren an fünf unterschiedlichen Gymnasien (sieben unterschiedliche Klassenverbände), durchgeführt. Alle Schüler_innen haben in der Grundschule mit Englisch angefangen, die meisten haben etwas später (in der 6. Klasse) mit einer weiteren Fremdsprache (Deutsch, Spanisch oder Französisch) begonnen. Zwei der Interviewpartner_innen haben erst am Gymnasium (9. Klasse) mit Deutsch angefangen. Von den insgesamt zwölf befragten Schüler_innen spricht die Mehrheit Schwedisch als Erstsprache, zwei davon sind zweisprachig aufgewachsen (Schwedisch und Türkisch).

Alle Interviews wurden halb strukturiert und leitfadengestützt durchgeführt[23]. Die Schüler_innen wurden dazu angeregt, ihre Meinungen, Assoziationen,

19 Jackson, Micke: *Deutsch macht Spaß! Oder?* Zuletzt gelesen am 08.01.2016 von http://dspace.mah.se/bitstream/handle/2043/1973/Examen%20MickeJackson.pdf?sequence=1 2005, S. 24–26.

20 Aguado, Karin: Triangulation. In: Settinieri, Julia et al. (Hrsg.): *Einführung in empirische Forschungsmethoden für Deutsch als Fremd- und Zweitsprache.* UTB: Paberborn 2014, S. 47–55, S. 53.

21 Hug, Theo/Poscheschnik, Gerald: *Empirisch forschen.* Verlag Huter & Roth KG: Wien, 2010, S. 101.

22 Beide Lehrpersonen arbeiten an Gymnasien, an denen Schwedisch und Englisch Pflichtfächer sind. Deutsch, Spanisch, Französisch, Italienisch und Japanisch bzw. Chinesisch ergänzen dieses Sprachlernangebot, sind aber kein Teil des obligatorischen Curriculums. An allen Schulen sind die Deutschgruppen durchmischt, d.h. dass Schüler_innen aus mehreren Klassen in einer Gruppe Deutsch lernen.

23 Daase, Andrea/Hinrichs, Beatrix/Settinieri, Julia: Befragung. In: Settinieri, Julia; Demirkaya, Sevilen; Feldmeier, Alexis; Gültekin-Karakoç, Nazan; Riemer, Claudia (Hrsg.): *Einführung in empirische Forschungsmethoden für Deutsch als Fremd- und Zweitsprache.* UTB: Paberborn, 2014, S. 103–122, hier S. 111.

Empfindungen zum Deutschen, ihre Motive für das Deutschlernen sowie ihre Einstellungen der Sprache und den Ländern gegenüber spontan in einer verbalen Reaktion auszudrücken. Beispielsweise wurden die Schüler_innen zu ihren Assoziationen zur Sprache und den amtlich deutschsprachigen Ländern befragt, und gebeten darüber zu reflektieren, woher diese Assoziationen kommen. Zudem wurde gefragt, was sie motiviert, Fremdsprachen allgemein und Deutsch im Spezifischen zu lernen, in welchen Situationen sie die deutsche Sprache verwenden, welche Rolle die deutsche Sprache in ihren Zukunftsplänen spielt und wie die Fremdsprachenwahl am Gymnasium getroffen wurde.

Die Analyse der Interviews erfolgte nach dem Prinzip der qualitativen Inhaltsanalyse nach Mayring (2010)[24]. Dabei wurde zunächst deduktiv vorgegangen. Dafür wurde ein Kategorienkatalog auf Grundlagen von zwei Studien – Riemer (2012) und Jackson (2005) (siehe Abschnitt 3) – entwickelt. Ergänzend dazu wurden nach einem ersten Materialdurchgang induktiv weitere Kategorien gebildet.

5 Ergebnisse

5.1 Einstellungen zur deutschen Sprache und zu den amtlich deutschsprachigen Ländern

Die vorgefundenen Einstellungen zur deutschen Sprache und zu den amtlich deutschsprachigen Ländern sind ein komplexes Zusammenspiel, das durch zahlreiche Faktoren beeinflusst wird. Diese sind einerseits extrinsisch, d.h. außerhalb der Schüler_innen angesiedelt, wie in der Schule, in Medien, bei Freunden, in Reisen oder in der Familie. Andererseits bestimmen aber auch persönliche Interessen und biographische Erfahrungen die Einstellungen. (intrinsische Faktoren). Als besonders zentral hat sich der Faktor Medien herausgestellt. Viele Schüler_innen gaben an, dass sich ihr Bild von der deutschen Sprache und dem amtlich deutschsprachigen Raum in erster Linie aus den von ihnen konsumierten Medien speist.

In Bezug auf die Sprache lässt sich sagen, dass sowohl die interviewten Lehrpersonen, als auch die Mehrheit der Schüler_innen die Ähnlichkeit zwischen Deutsch und Schwedisch, vor allem auf der lexikalischen Ebene, betonten. Laut einer Schülerin sei Deutsch „50 % Schwedisch". Dank dieser Ähnlichkeit empfinden es viele als einfach, die deutsche Sprache zu lernen und zu verstehen.

---

24 Mayring, Philipp: *Qualitative Inhaltsanalyse. Grundlagen und Techniken. 11. aktualisierte und überarbeitete Auflage.* Weinheim & Basel: Beltz, 2010.

Andererseits gilt Deutsch laut beiden interviewten Lehrerpersonen aufgrund der Grammatik als „schwierig". Diesbezüglich waren unterschiedliche Aussagen seitens der Schüler_innen festzustellen. Nur vier der zwölf interviewten Schüler_innen assoziierten Deutsch mit Grammatik. Für einige war dies mit Schwierigkeiten verbunden und daher eher negativ konnotiert. Andere fanden aber gerade Grammatik spannend und scheinen Deutsch deswegen zu mögen.

Die Phonetik der deutschen Sprache wurde in allen Interviews thematisiert. Laut den Lehrpersonen reagieren schwedische Schüler_innen auf die phonetischen Besonderheiten des Deutschen und empfinden es als grob oder abgehackt. Ähnliches war den Schüler_inneninterviews zu entnehmen: Deutsch höre sich „schnell", „grob", „aggressiv" oder „hart" an. Als Grund für diese negativen Assoziationen wurde von einem Teil der Schüler_innen der Zweite Weltkrieg und das daraus entstandene Image der Deutschen in Schweden angeführt. Andere fanden Erklärungen in der Häufigkeit von „ch"-Lauten. In diesem Zusammenhang ist es erwähnenswert, dass laut einigen Schüler_innen diese Wahrnehmung in Schweden weit verbreitet sei; daher wurde sie als „Vorurteil" gegenüber der Sprache bezeichnet. Viele der Interviewten betonen in diesem Zusammenhang, dass Deutsch für sie selbst „schön" klingt, und drückten eine positive Einstellung bzw. Sympathie für die Sprache aus. So erzählte eine interviewte Schülerin beispielsweise Folgendes: „Ich finde, es ist sehr sehr schön und es ist so eine sehr gemütliche Sprache, denn ich fühle mich so wie zu Hause, wenn ich es höre."

Was die Einstellungen den Ländern gegenüber anbelangt, so fällt in allen Interviews auf, dass das Deutschlandbild dominierte, auch wenn immer nach den amtlich deutschsprachigen Ländern gefragt wurde. Daher wurde explizit nach Österreich und der Schweiz gefragt. Stereotype Bilder kamen in jedem Interview vor. Beispielsweise wurden deutsche Automarken, Autobahnen, Fußball, traditionelle Speisen (vor allem Wurst, aber auch Schnitzel), Berge und Skifahren in Verbindung mit Österreich und der Schweiz genannt. Die Schweiz sei sehr teuer, Österreich sei Mozarts Land. Vor allem Deutsche wurden von einigen der Befragten als sehr laut beschrieben. Allerdings ist es erwähnenswert, dass viele Schüler_innen ihre Assoziationen selbst als verbreitete Stereotype bezeichneten. Eine kleinere Gruppe assoziierte die amtlich deutschsprachigen Länder mit ihrer Familie und/oder ihren Interessen wie Reisen, Fußball oder Sprachen.

Eine sehr verbreitete Assoziation vor allem in Zusammenhang mit Deutschland war der Zweite Weltkrieg. Die Schüler_innen betonten, dass dieser keine Rolle bei ihren Einstellungen den Ländern und/oder der Sprache gegenüber spielt, weil er sich vor vielen Jahren ereignet habe und die Menschen von heute anders seien. Zudem wurde über die Rolle der Medien reflektiert. Als Beispiele wurden Filme genannt, bei denen ein Deutscher die Rolle des Schurken mit einer besonders aggressiven Sprache und Intonation übernimmt, wodurch das Bild von Deutsch-Sprecher_innen als „bad guys" reproduziert wurde. Vielen Interviews ist eine kritische Reflexion bezüglich dieses von Medien gezeichneten Bildes von Deutsch-Sprechenden zu entnehmen. Einerseits wurden Stereotype reproduziert, andererseits distanzierten sich die Schüler_innen davon. Die Interviewten betonten, dass diese stereotypen Bilder durch persönlichen Kontakt, Reisen und die Auseinandersetzung mit Sprache und Kultur dekonstruiert wurden.

5.2 Motive für die Wahl der deutschen Sprache

In Schweden lässt sich die allgemeine Tendenz feststellen, dass Spanisch die größte Popularität unter den Schüler_innen genießt, gefolgt von Französisch und Deutsch[25]. Als möglichen Grund für die steigende Beliebtheit des Spanischen auf Kosten des Deutschen sehen beide Lehrpersonen die Tatsache, dass die amtlich deutschsprachigen Länder nicht zu den typischsten Urlaubszielen der Schüler_innen gehören. Eine andere Ursache dafür könne mit den Englischkenntnissen der Schüler_innen zusammenhängen, welche für eine Reise nach Deutschland ausreichend seien. Gegen die Wahl der deutschen Sprache spreche laut den Lehrpersonen außerdem das Image einer sehr grammatiklastigen, schwierigen Sprache.

Allerdings gaben einige Schüler_innen an, großes Interesse an Grammatik zu haben, was einer ihrer Gründe war, warum sie sich für Deutsch entschieden haben. Grammatik wurde als eine Herausforderung beschrieben, die zum Lernen motiviert. Weiters wurde Deutsch als eine schöne, fröhliche Sprache beschrieben, was ebenso die Lernmotivation steigert. Für eine Reihe der Befragten war die Ähnlichkeit zwischen Schwedisch und Deutsch und die daraus resultierenden Lernvorteile ausschlaggebend. Dies bestätigten auch die Lehrpersonen. Sie gaben an, dass laut ihrer Wahrnehmung Eltern oft ihren Kindern raten, Deutsch zu wählen, weil es „am leichtesten" sei und man viele Wörter aufgrund der Ähnlichkeit zum Schwedischen „gratis" bekomme. Außerdem haben viele Eltern Deutsch gelernt und können bei Hausaufgaben helfen.

Beide Lehrer_innen gaben zudem an, dass viele Schüler_innen Deutsch wegen der Familie lernen. In ihren Klassen gebe es Schüler_innen, deren Verwandte entweder in einem amtlich deutschsprachigen Land wohnen, oder aus einem dieser Länder stammen. Die Mehrheit der interviewten Schüler_innen betonte auch die zentrale Rolle der Familie bei der Entscheidung, Deutsch zu

---

25 Vgl. Petersson 2012.

lernen. Durch das Lernen der deutschen Sprache scheinen die Schüler_innen eine Verbindung zu ihrer Familie aufrechtzuerhalten. Deutsch zu können wird als Teil der Familienidentität verstanden.

Neben der Familie wurde als weiteres Motiv auch der instrumentelle Nutzen von Deutschkenntnissen genannt. Deutsch zu können wird als wertvoll angesehen und es wird davon ausgegangen, dass Deutschkenntnisse aufgrund der Wirtschaftsbeziehungen zwischen Deutschland und Schweden „Konkurrenzfähigkeit" am Arbeitsmarkt mit sich bringen. Vielfach würden deshalb Eltern ihren Kindern empfehlen, Deutsch zu wählen. Mehrere Schüler_innen entschieden sich aber auch unabhängig vom Rat ihrer Eltern aufgrund dieses instrumentellen Nutzens für Deutsch. Für viele ist die Rolle der Deutschkenntnisse zentral für ihre Pläne, zu reisen und die deutschsprachigen Länder zu entdecken. Des Weiteren berichteten einige, dass Deutsch eine mehr oder weniger wichtige Rolle für das künftige Studium und/oder den Beruf spielen wird. Die Pläne der Schüler_innen unterschieden sich zwar in ihrer Konkretheit, von allen wurde aber die Möglichkeit betont, die Deutschkenntnisse in den amtlich deutschsprachigen Ländern zu verwenden, dort zu arbeiten und/oder zu studieren. Auch die interviewten Lehrpersonen erwähnten, dass Deutschkenntnisse mit instrumentellem Nutzen verbunden werden. Insgesamt erachten sie dieses Motiv aber im Vergleich zu den anderen Motiven für die Wahl der deutschen Sprache als weniger ausschlaggebend.

Ein weiterer Motivationsfaktor, der in den Interviews genannt wurde, ist das Interesse an Kultur und Sport aus den deutschsprachigen Ländern. Zudem wurde auch der Wunsch, mit deutschsprachigen Freunden zu kommunizieren, als Motivationsfaktor genannt. Vergangene und/oder künftige Reisen in ein amtlich deutschsprachiges Land sind bei einigen auch ein Beweggrund, Deutsch zu lernen.

Einige der Schüler_innen hinterließen den Eindruck, Deutsch unter anderem deswegen gewählt zu haben, weil die anderen Fremdsprachen nicht attraktiv genug waren. Zum einen wirkte Deutsch für viele im Vergleich zu Spanisch und Französisch am einfachsten erlernbar, zum anderen fühlten sie sich nicht von der Klassenatmosphäre im Spanischunterricht angesprochen. Ein Problem der Spanischgruppen sei die Größe, ein weiteres sei die nicht ausreichende Motivation mancher Schüler_innen. Die Interviewten äußerten die Vermutung, dass der Unterricht dadurch beeinträchtigt werde, weswegen sie eine bewusste Wahl gegen Spanisch getroffen haben. Einige empfanden die anderen angebotenen Fremdsprachen (meistens Französisch und Spanisch) als nicht „schön".

Aus der Analyse der sprachlichen Hintergründe der interviewten Schüler_innen geht hervor, dass die Mehrheit schon in der Grundschule mit einer

Fremdsprache angefangen hat. Einige haben Spanisch gelernt und sich im Gymnasium für einen Wechsel entschieden, möglicherweise aus den oben genannten Gründen. Andere haben Deutsch als erste Fremdsprache gelernt und berichteten, dass sie motiviert waren, weiterzumachen, da sie schon viel konnten und es sinnlos wäre, diese Kenntnisse nicht weiterzuentwickeln. Hier kann von einer Kontinuität in der Entwicklung der persönlichen Fremdsprachenkenntnisse gesprochen werden.

6 Conclusio

Insgesamt zeigt sich, dass die Mehrheit der interviewten Schüler_innen die Wahl der deutschen Sprache als eine eigene Wahl betrachtet. Ausschlaggebend waren verschiedene interne und externe Faktoren:

- Familie, Familientradition, Familienidentität;
- Ähnlichkeit mit der schwedischen Sprache, leichtere Erlernbarkeit;
- Grammatik;
- Deutsch als eine schöne Sprache;
- instrumenteller Nutzen der Deutschkenntnisse für Reisen, Studium und Beruf;
- Wunsch, auf Deutsch zu kommunizieren;
- eigene Interessen, die mit der Sprache und/oder den Ländern in Verbindung stehen;
- Weniger attraktive Angebote für andere Fremdsprachen.

All diese Faktoren stehen in engem Zusammenhang mit der Person und der Biographie der Lernenden. Den Aussagen der Interviewten ist zu entnehmen, dass die Entscheidung, Deutsch zu lernen, selbstständig und bewusst getroffen wurde, nachdem diverse Faktoren in Erwägung gezogen worden waren. Außerdem vermittelten sie den Eindruck, die Sprache mit Freude zu erlernen, da diese oft mit ihren eigenen Interessen in Verbindung steht. Aus diesem Grund kann angenommen werden, dass das Deutschlernen ein bewusster, motivationsgeleiteter Prozess ist, der zu einem Bestandteil der Schüler_innenidentität wird. Zudem soll die Bereitschaft der Interviewten hervorgehoben werden, ihre Deutschkenntnisse zu praktizieren und sich mit der Kultur der deutschsprachigen Länder auseinanderzusetzen. Sei es für berufliche oder private Zwecke, der Dialog durch und in der deutschen Sprache ist ein Zukunftsziel aller Befragten.

Die Studie hat gezeigt, dass Deutschlernende in Schweden eine Verbindung zwischen ihrer Erstsprache Schwedisch und der Zielsprache Deutsch sehen – die Sprachen sind „im Dialog" und das motiviert zum Lernen. Der „Dialog der

Sprachen" geht Hand in Hand mit dem „Dialog der Kulturen", denn die Auseinandersetzung der Schüler_innen mit Deutsch ist nicht nur eine Auseinandersetzung mit grammatikalischen und lexikalischen Strukturen, sondern sie ist auch ein Ausdruck der persönlichen Interessen an den Zielsprachenkulturen.

Bibliographie

Aguado, Karin: Triangulation. In: Settinieri, Julia et al. (Hrsg.): *Einführung in empirische Forschungsmethoden für Deutsch als Fremd- und Zweitsprache.* UTB: Paberborn 2014 S. 47–55.

Daase, Andrea/Hinrichs, Beatrix/Settinieri, Julia: Befragung. In: Settinieri, Julia; Demirkaya, Sevilen; Feldmeier, Alexis; Gültekin-Karakoç, Nazan; Riemer, Claudia (Hrsg.): *Einführung in empirische Forschungsmethoden für Deutsch als Fremd- und Zweitsprache.* UTB: Paberborn, 2014, S. 103–122.

Dörnyei, Zoltan: *Motivation in second and foreign language learning.* In: Language Teaching (31) July 1998 S. 117–135.

Dörnyei, Zoltán: *Motivational Strategies in the Language Classroom.* University Press: Cambridge 2001.

Gardner, Robert: *Social Psychology and Second Language Learning. The Role of Attitudes and Motivation.* Edward Arnold: London 1985.

Jackson, Micke: *Deutsch macht Spaß! Oder?* Zuletzt gelesen am 08.01.2016 von http://dspace.mah.se/bitstream/handle/2043/1973/Examen%20MickeJackson.pdf?sequence=1 2005.

Kleppin, Karin: Der Faktor Motivation in der individuellen Sprachlernberatung. In: Küppers, Almut/Quetz, Jürgen (Hrsg.): *Motivation Revisited. Festschrift für Gert Solmecke.* Lit Verlag: Berlin 2006 S. 57–68.

Mayring, Philipp: *Qualitative Inhaltsanalyse. Grundlagen und Techniken. 11. aktualisierte und überarbeitete Auflage.* Beltz: Weinheim/Basel 2010.

Petersson, Kenny: *Tyska förlorar mark i Europa. Statistiska centralbyrån.* Zuletzt gelesen am 06.01.2016 von http://www.scb.se/sv_/Hitta-statistik/Artiklar/Tyska-spraket-forlorar-mark-i-Europa/ 2012.

Riemer, Claudia: Motivation in der empirischen Fremdsprachenforschung. In: Küppers, Almut/Quetz, Jürgen (Hrsg.): *Motivation Revisited. Festschrift für Gert Solmecke.* Lit Verlag: Berlin 2006 S. 35–48.

Riemer, Claudia: Motivation. In: Barkowski, Hans/Krumm, Hans-Jürgen (Hrsg.): *Fachlexikon Deutsch als Fremd- und Zweitsprache.* A. Franke Verlag: Tübingen/Basel 2010, S. 219–220.

Riemer, Claudia: „Warum Deutsch (noch) gelernt wird – Motivationsforschung und Deutsch als Fremdsprache". In: Barkowski, Hans et al. (Hrsg.): *Deutsch bewegt. Entwicklungen in der Auslandsgermanistik und Deutsch als Fremd- und Zweitsprache.* Schneider: Baltmannsweiler 2012, S. 327–340.

Sherif, Carolyn/Sherif, Muzafer: *Social Psychology.* Harper & Row: New York 1969.

Städtler, Thomas: *Lexikon der Psychologie.* Wörterbuch. Handbuch. Studienbuch. Kröner: Stuttgart 1998.

Tendzeric, Biljana/Töttrup, Sara: *Tyska med elevers ögon. En studie om elevers attityd till ämnet tyska och dess undervisning.* 2008 Zuletzt gelesen am 21.01.2016 von http://www.diva-portal.org/smash/get/diva2:238505/FULLTEXT01.pdf.

Wessén, Elias: *Om det tyska inflytandet på svenskt språk under medeltiden.* 3. Auflage. Kungl. Boktryckeriet: Stockholm 1970

Valerio Fidenzi

Reporting remoteness: Tristan da Cunha in the British press (1816–1949)

Abstract: The present chapter investigates selected instances of dialogue between the United Kingdom and Tristan da Cunha, a British Overseas Territory in the South Atlantic Ocean. More specifically, the chapter examines how Tristan da Cunha was represented in the British newspapers between 1816 and 1949, and therefore what kind of image of this island did the Anglophone press contribute to shaping. To this aim, a corpus of 163 texts has been compiled and all the texts analysed using Corpus-Assisted Discourse Study (CADS). Besides showing the little visibility given by the press to the island, the analysis of the data brings to the fore both the rhetoric of isolation that inevitably adorns discourse on Tristan da Cunha, and a tendency to idealise the life of the islanders that at times fails to bring to the reader's attention the severe hardships that the emerging community was facing in the early decades of colonisation. It is only at the turn of the century that more visibility is given to the island, and that prejudices and stereotypes on its population start to be challenged, but the thunder of two world conflicts ends up pushing, once again, Tristan da Cunha into oblivion and isolation.

1 Tristan da Cunha and the British press, 1810s–1940s

Tristan da Cunha is a small island of volcanic origin, home, at present, of 257 islanders.[1] If we had to locate its coordinates, we would find ourselves in the middle of the South Atlantic Ocean, about 2,300 kilometres from the nearest inhabited place: the island of St Helena. No wonder, Tristan da Cunha welcomes its visitors by advertising itself as the remotest inhabited island in the world.

The island was formally annexed to the British Crown in 1816, and permanently settled by six people including a Scottish corporal named William Glass that would become the first Administrator.[2] Starting from that moment, increasingly heterogeneous groups of people contributed to the colonisation of Tristan da Cunha, to the point that, at the end of the 19th century, the island had already served as a contact zone for people from Britain, South Africa, Denmark, Holland, St Helena, North America and Italy. Although the outcome of this isolated contact scenario has extensively been analysed from a number

---

1   http://tristandc.com/familynews.php (last accessed in November 2017).
2   Brander, Jan: *Tristan da Cunha 1506–1902*. Allen & Unwin: London 1940.

of perspectives and scientific viewpoints (for the linguistic one, see Anne Zettersten's pioneering publication,[3] as well as Daniel Schreier's monograph[4] and paper[5] co-authored with Peter Trudgill), no study has been conducted on the representation of the island and of its people in the British press.

This chapter aims at investigating a case of unequal dialogue between unequal communities,[6] meaning Britain's viewpoint on Tristan da Cunha as transpiring from the news pieces published between 1816, the year of annexation of the island, and 1949, the year that symbolically marks the end of the non-industrialised part of the history of Tristan da Cunha. The underlying assumption is that these texts, far from being sheer reporting of events, contributed to a broader discourse on discovery and exploration of the other that ended up shaping an image of Tristan da Cunha that might not perfectly adhere to reality, or might not be the one needed by the community. This is relevant especially considering the great deal of effort devoted by the Tristanians to surviving periods of extreme isolation, thus to make the outside world aware of its needs, be it goods, provisions or even shelter when the volcano erupted back in the 1960s. Newspapers, as means of popularised knowledge dissemination, had the potential of making news on the island resonate throughout Britain, therefore of calling for aid when the island needed it the most.

As for the situation of the British press in this period, the first half of the 19th century saw the British newspaper landscape boosted by the reduction and, in 1855, final abolition of the stamp duties. This, combined with remarkable technological breakthroughs, caused an explosion in the circulation of newspapers. Then, towards the beginning of the 20th century, the idea of the press as a Fourth Estate with a respectable place in the political system started gaining power.[7] Needless to say, this had significant consequences for the ideological influence

3   Zettersten, Anne: *The English of Tristan da Cunha*. Gleerup, Lund Studies in English, Vol. 3: Lund 1969.
4   Schreier, Daniel: *Isolation and language change: Contemporary and sociohistorical evidence from Tristan da Cunha English*. Palgrave Macmillan: Basingstoke 2003.
5   Schreier, Daniel & Peter Trudgill: *The segmental phonology of nineteenth-century Tristan da Cunha English: Convergence and local innovation*. English Language and Linguistics, 10 (2006), pp. 119–141.
6   It is unequal because, more than a dialogue in itself, it can be considered a monologue. It involves unequal communities because on the one side there is Britain, therefore the motherland, and on the other side its remotest and least populated outpost.
7   Bös, Birte: *From 1760 to 1960: Diversification and popularization,* in R. Facchinetti, N. Brownlees, B. Bös and U. Fries: *News as changing texts: Corpora, methodologies and analysis.* Cambridge University Press: Cambridge 2015 (2nd ed.), pp. 91–143.

of newspapers on society, thus for the representation and reception of far away cultures in the news pieces.

2 The study: corpus, aims and methodologies

The present study reports the quantitative and qualitative analysis of a number of British news pieces on Tristan da Cunha, thus seeking to answer the following questions: How relevant is Tristan in the British press? How is life on the island reported? Is there any change in the representation of Tristan over time? What image of Tristan and of its community do the news pieces contribute to shaping?

In order to assemble the corpus, the *British Library Newspaper Part II: 1800–1900*[8] archive and *The British Newspaper Archive*[9] (both available online to registered users and institutions) have been screened for the pairs "Tristan" AND "Acunha" and "Tristan" AND "Cunha" featured in each title of the articles published between 1816 and 1949. The pairs were chosen according to the two spelling variants popular in the centuries covered by the study: Tristan D'Acunha (which was later dropped) and Tristan da Cunha. The screening has yielded a total of 163 texts for 46.625 running words, divided into 18 texts (7.411 words) published between 1816 and 1899 and 145 texts (39.214 words) published between 1900 and 1949. In order to obtain a fully machine-readable corpus, the resulting 163 texts have been transcribed and converted from.*pdf* into.*txt* format, and then analysed using *Sketch Engine*,[10] an online corpus manager and analysis tool allowing for search specificities relevant to the present study.

The study finds its methodological base in the relatively recent but prolific tradition of Corpus-Assisted Discourse Studies (CADS), a branch of linguistics first formulated in 1996 and based on the synergic use of corpus linguistics and discourse analysis. This approach to the study of language inherits from corpus linguistics "a bottom-up, data-driven analysis that relies on a large amount on linguistic data, [but combining it with a] discourse analysis approach, stressing the importance of […] looking at the context outside the concordance lines".[11]

---

8   The archive includes regional and local newspapers published in Britain during the 19th century.
9   The archive gives access to more than 200 newspaper titles from every part of the British Isles dating from the 1700s.
10 Available at: https://www.sketchengine.co.uk/.
11 Marchi, Anna/Taylor Charlotte: "Establishing the EU: The representation of Europe in the press in 1993 and 2005". In: Jucker, Andreas H./Schreier Daniel/Hundt Marianne (eds.) *Corpora: Pragmatics and Discourse: Papers from the 29th International*

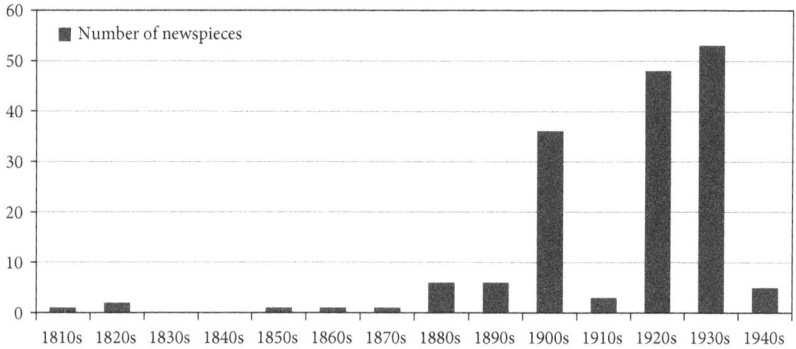

Graphic 1: *Decade of publication of the news pieces*

3 Findings

Overall, the small number of texts yielded by the archives (163 texts over a time period of 133 years) is significant of the poor visibility of Tristan da Cunha in the British press. While the numerical distribution of the 163 texts is highlighted in Graphic 1, the following are the most involved newspapers (the number of articles published by each newspaper is specified within brackets): *The Scotsman* (28), *The Morning Post* (13), *Belfast Newsletter* (9), *Western Morning News* (8), *Portsmouth Evening News* (7).

Besides showing the most relevant newspapers, the short list above offers a snapshot of the main cities in which news on Tristan da Cunha was published in this period. As the newspaper titles themselves suggest, news on Tristan comes from all over the United Kingdom, from south to north, from Portsmouth to Edinburgh, passing through London and Belfast.

As for the numerical distribution of the texts over the 14 decades, shown in Graphic 1, this follows a gradual increase that is only interrupted by a sharp rise at the turn of the century, and by two lows in the 1910s and the 1940s, owing to the effects of the two World Wars.

Conference on English Language Research on Computerized Corpora (ICAME 29). Rodopi: Amsterdam et. al. 2009, 203–226.

Tab. 1: *Frequency lists of* Sub-corpus_800 *and* Sub-corpus_900

Sub-corpus_800		Sub-corpus_900	
Lemma[a]	Frequency	Lemma	Frequency
They/Their/ Them	148	They/Their/Them	555
Island	65	Tristan	432
He/His	59	Island	407
Tristan	52	He/His	327
I	49	Cunha	306
Ship	40	Will	205
Very	32	Islander	157
We	29	Ship	138
Man	27	Year	118
Acunha	26	I	107
Visit	23	We	105
Year	22	Make	103
Green	21	Very	102
Her	21	Send	95
Make	21	Mail	94

[a] According to the definition provided by *Sketch Engine* (see the definition at https://www.sketchengine.co.uk/my_keywords/lemma/, last accessed in November 2017), "lemma is the basic form of a word, typically the form found in dictionaries. [...] searching for lemma *go* will find *go, goes, went, going, gone*".

3.1 Computer-based analysis

In order to grasp general changes in the way news on Tristan da Cunha is reported over more than a century, the corpus has been divided into two sub-corpora, *Sub-corpus_800*, dating from 1816 to 1899, and *Sub-corpus_900*, dating from 1900 to 1949, and two frequency lists of both have been made using *Sketch Engine*, so that each sub-corpus can be considered the other's reference sub-corpus, without the need for an external reference corpus. The frequency lists in Tab. 1 show the fifteen most frequent content words (plus other relevant words like personal pronouns) in the two sub-corpora under consideration. This is a worthwhile starting point, because word lists are fair pictures of the main topics dealt with in corpora, as well as, thanks to the collocations offered by the tool, of their use in context. Moreover, a comparison between the two is useful in grasping possible changes in the way of reporting the news.

The high frequency of the personal pronouns *they* and *I* in both *Sub-corpus_800* and *Sub-corpus_900* is revealing of the way in which pronouns are used in the articles to draw borders between social groups: the British group on the one side (*I/we*) and the Tristanians on the other (*they*). It is thus noteworthy that the Tristanians seem to be perceived as a self-standing social group with their own identity already in the first decades of the 19th century, notwithstanding the fact that most of them were living in the United Kingdom until a few decades before. From a merely communal point of view, this might have helped the affirmation of the Tristanians' community identity in the eyes of Britain, because, as the analysed texts suggest, the British were not perceived as British anymore, but rather (and already) as Tristanians.

As for the personal pronouns *her* and *he*, the former is predictably mostly used in collocations with *Majesty*, while the latter is almost exclusively used to refer to William Glass, the island's first Administrator, who stands out as Tristan da Cunha's only "flesh and bone" person (besides the second Administrator Peter Green), thus with a name and a surname, and as recipient of the personal pronoun.

The adverb *very* is of interest because of the evaluation it carries. This is particularly true if we consider the fact that the collocation with the adjective *interesting* (also evaluative) is the most recurring one. As the following examples show, the evaluative form *very interesting* is used both for the settlement and for reports on the settlement.

(1) … contains the following very interesting account from Tristan d'Acuna…[12]
(2) … claims attention for the very interesting settlement on Tristan d'Acuna…[13]
(3) … the history of this very interesting little settlement is most…[14]

It is worth highlighting, however, that this interest is always triggered by the everlasting fascination exerted by the isolation of Tristan da Cunha, and by remote places in general. As the discourse analysis in Section 3.2 shows, this results in an idealisation that ends up paving the way to a simplified image of the island that, in turn, fails to bring to the fore the remarkable achievements of the community. Moreover, only rarely is the adverb *very* used to refer to the Tristanians' most urgent needs, such as cloth, tobacco, sugar, tea, coffee and other goods they could never produce themselves.

---

12 *The Standard*, 29/12/1829.
13 *The Royal Nornwall Gazette, Falmouth Packet, and General Advertiser,* 05/06/1857.
14 *Ibid.*

The concordances of *man* show that the lemma is mostly used in the plural form *men* to provide information concerning the number of people inhabiting the island, which is one of the most frequent topics in the news pieces. When the word is in the singular form *man*, it is always used to refer either to the island's first administrator William Glass or to the second administrator Peter Green (whose surname scores thirteenth in the list of lemmas of *Sub-corpus_800*). No direct reference is made to the other islanders, who are mostly perceived and reported as a whole entity. Of course, this picture is an oversimplification that goes hand in hand with the little relevance that, more generally speaking, the British newspapers in the corpus give to Tristan da Cunha. Nevertheless, the community identity and the sense of in-group belonging and unity do not seem to be concepts that would be of any problem to the present-day islanders, who are particularly aware of the importance of being united as a community.

Finally, the lemmas *ship*, *visit* and *year* are significant both of the strong nautical tradition of Tristan da Cunha and of the newsworthiness criteria applied to it: it is the visit of a British ship that makes the island newsworthy, just as it is the visit of a British ship that marks the passage of time on the island.

What the list pertaining to *Sub-corpus_900* shows is that changes in the way of reporting the news at the turn of the century are not particularly significant, at least with reference to lexis. Besides the apparent affirmation of a less personalised kind of writing (a change signalled by the decreased use of *I* and *we*), and besides a slightly different prioritisation of the lemmas, the main difference between the two sub-corpora is the prominent presence of the modal verb *will* (see section 3.1.1), as well as of *send* and *mail*, which are exemplifying of the increasing prominence given to the need of keeping the interested reader up to date about the British ships calling at Tristan, thus aware of the possibility of sending mails and goods to the inhabitants. This is because the first decades of the twentieth century were a period of hardship and growing isolation for the islanders, who, at one stage, "had no communication whatsoever with the outside world for more than three years".[15] When the seriousness of this situation was understood, newspapers in Britain started prioritising the links of connection between the United Kingdom and its Overseas Territory, thus raising awareness of the possibility to send supplies to the Tristanians. This, however, sometimes meant falling in the trap of overshadowing everything that was not

---

15 Schreier, Daniel/Lavarello-Schreier, Karen: *Tristan da Cunha and the Tristanians.* Battlebridge Publications: London 2011, p. 38.

naval connections between the UK and the island, as the content analysis of
some articles suggests (see 3.2).

3.1.1 The hidden evaluation of the modal verb *will*

The presence of the modal verb *will* in the frequency list of *Sub-corpus_900*
brings to the fore the fact that, besides being a particularly frequent lemma, *will*
is also the most prominent modal verb in the corpus. Furthermore, the analysis
of its concordance lines yields interesting patterns with reference to the subjects
of *will*, which can be divided into three macro-groups with striking differences
in terms of distribution: (A) the subjects of *will* are both abstract and material
things such as parcels, mails, ships, stores and opportunities; (B) the subjects
of *will* are people other than the Tristanians, such as officials, commanders
and priests; (C) the subjects of *will* are Tristan da Cunha and the Tristanians.
These three groups account respectively for 68 % (A), 19 % (B) and 13 % (C) of
occurrences, meaning that only 28 times out of 219 is Tristan (and its people) the
subject of this modal verb *will*.

What is more, even when the Tristanians are the subjects of *will*, some
distinctions need to be made, resulting in the emergence of a majority of
both instances of negative evaluation and representations of the Tristanians as
recipients at the mercy of external factors, therefore taking the semantic role of
experiencer carried by the flow of events, of which they receive and undergo the
effects. This is well illustrated in the examples from 4 to 6.

(4) … it is considered that either they will have to be so moved, possibly to
     Australia…[16]
(5) … they will never develop that form of self reliance and ambition…[17]
(6) … their naturally lazy natures will further deteriorate…[18]

Only twice do the concordances of *will* feature the Tristanians as both subjects
and semantic agents of the sentence. In both occasions (examples 7 and 8) the
Tristanians are reported to be refusing the prospect of having to permanently
leave the island.

(7) … they will not consent to leave the island…[19]
(8) … we will never leave Tristan.[20]

---

16 *The Moring Post*, 15/12/1886.
17 *Littlehampton Gazette*, 11/5/1923.
18 *Ibid.*
19 *The Scotsman*, 4/10/1907.

Overall, it is the Tristanians' attachment to their land to stand out as their only overtly expressed will, and this is particularly fitting (although not significant in terms of frequency).

3.2 Discourse analysis

A qualitative reading of the texts highlights a slow but relevant change in the representation of Tristan da Cunha over time, a change that is not overtly expressed by the frequency lists of the two sub-corpora.

In *Sub-corpus_800*, the discourse on discovery and early settlement that introduces the reader to this remote islet goes hand in hand with the reporting of fascinating stories, such as the Duke of Edinburgh's visit to the island in 1867 and the Queen's gift to the island's Administrator in the 1890s. It is worth noticing that these stories, told with plenty of details and descriptions, are both related to a very strong instance of contact between Britain and Tristan da Cunha, which entails the most prominent figures in the Monarchy paying a visit or sending tributes to the island. This is revealing of the newsworthiness of Tristan da Cunha in the 19th century, meaning of how more visibility is given to the island when a direct contact is established with Britain. However, the links that connect Tristan da Cunha with the United Kingdom are there even without the Duke's visit and the Queen's gift: not only is Tristan a British dependency, but the island is also mostly inhabited by people who, no more than few decades before the publication of these news pieces, were living in England and Scotland. In any case, the reports to which more prominence is given are inevitably those two, and the story of the Duke's visit, featured in *The Sheffield & Rotherham Independent* (3/12/1867), inevitably reminds a fairy tale. The title itself reads THE DUKE OF EDINBURGH'S VISIT TO TRISTAN D'ACUNHA. A HAPPY FAMILY and when the event is remembered, a couple of decades later, by *The Standard* the tale becomes even more involving, with a fairy tale resolution[21], and the recurring happy family frame testifying to the fact that discourse on Tristan da Cunha in the 1800s is somehow idealised, to say the least. This is how, for instance, *The*

---

20 *Bellshill Speaker*, 6/4/1928.
21 The Duke voluntarily took charge of a bundle from Mr. Green and had it delivered to Capetown, where his daughters were living in the service of the Government House. When Mr. Green's daughters opened the bundle, they found that the Duke had left them some money to improve their life conditions.

Royal Cornwall Gazette, Falmouth Packet, and General Advertiser describes the community:

> Happily, they could appreciate the value of Religion as the bond of Society, and the foundation as well of present comfort as of future hope, and as in the ancient patriarchal dispensation the prince and the priest were one [...]. Their numbers have increased, but they have always continued a simple-minded, united, religious community. [...] The history of this very interesting little settlement is most instructive, and suggests matter for serious consideration [...].[22]

In contrast to this naïf representation, the island was actually undergoing a period of isolation and extreme hardship in the second half of the 19th century. This alternation between no news and simplified representations of facts was only broken in 1886, when *The Star* reported that the inhabitants were in a state of starvation and needing provisions.[23] As mentioned, it was only when the seriousness of the situation was understood that the British Government took the decision of sending annual supply ships to the community. This improved the islanders' conditions for some time and inevitably engaged the press' interest.

At the turn of the century, despite an evident boost in the publication of articles related to Tristan, news on the island seems to be, at first, still bound to a kind of discourse centred on its uniquely isolated condition and ignoring more important matters. It is only towards the beginning of the 1910s that it starts showing diverging tendencies.

On the one hand, texts start to appear that, more than news pieces, can be considered notifications on the naval connections between the UK and the island, and whose aim is to inform people in Britain of the possibility of sending mails and products to the islanders. These notifications are usually very short, they explain the presence of *send* and *mail* in the frequency list, and represent the main reason why *Sub-corpus_900*, although being comprised of far more news pieces than *Sub-corpus_800* (145 against 18), has a proportionally much smaller number of words, meaning an average of 270 words per article against the 411 of *Sub-corpus_800*. However short and concise, these kinds of notifications do fulfil the scope and guarantee the service of keeping people in the UK up to date about the ships calling at Tristan in the near future, and therefore informed about the possibility of supporting the islanders by sending them provisions.

On the other hand, a numerous group of articles does break the idealised frame typical of the 19th century by introducing more detailed descriptions of

22 *The Royal Cornwall Gazette, Falmouth Packet, and General Advertiser*, 5/6/1857.
23 *The Star*, 18/9/1886.

the island customs and traditions, but also of the difficulties that life on an isolated island entails. On 10th February 1932, the *Western Daily Press* published an article titled COURTING DAYS IN TRISTAN DA CUNHA, illustrating a traditional wedding day on the island. Few days later, the *Belfast Newsletter* went further on in describing similar traditions and also attempted to challenge some prejudices that had started to circulate on the islanders: "The idea that constant intermarriage had produced degenerate race is proved to have been definitely wrong".[24] This positive trend was then followed by other newspapers like the *Edinburgh Evening News*, which, in the same year, published an article containing a section titled POPULAR ERRORS and challenging similar beliefs: "Tristan is a healthy place, and has no infectious disease. The only serious illness occurs after a ship has called!".[25] Finally, the end of the non-industrialised part of the history of Tristan da Cunha is beautifully portrayed in the last article of the corpus, published at the end of 1949 and featuring some remarks that end up casting a new and more realistic light on the history of Tristan da Cunha until 1949, thus challenging, once again, some prejudices and stereotypes that had been lingering for more than one century:

> So ends the long romance of the free and independent Tristan community, and there will not be lacking those who lament that one more little outpost has been drawn into the net of commercial life. But those who have lived among them will realise that the existence was less rosy than popular imagination supposed, and there is no doubt that the islanders themselves prefer the comparative security of employment for wages, with a well-filled store at which they can spend their money, to a hand-to-mouth existence relieved only by the arrival of the annual supply ship, which itself did not always put in an appearance. Many times, as the old minds can tell you, they have been reduced to living on "beer and taters", which means potatoes and nothing else and there have been times when these have been none too plentiful either.[26]

It is thus a generally positive trend to emerge out of a content analysis of the news pieces published in the first half of the 20th century. As seen in the graphic showing the numerical distribution of articles (Graphic 1), however, when the thunder of the two World Wars took the world's and press' attention, Tristan da Cunha was pushed, once again, into oblivion and isolation, suggesting that its greater problem was still primarily one of visibility.

---

24 *Belfast Newsletter*, 22/2/1932.
25 *Edinburgh Evening News*, 23/4/1932.
26 *Yorkshire Post and Leeds Intelligencer*, 17/11/1949.

4 Conclusions

This chapter has illustrated a case of unequal dialogue between unequal cultures, exemplified by UK news pieces about the island of Tristan da Cunha. Specifically, the analysis of the data has brought to the fore two main issues.

The first is a problem of quantity, therefore of visibility, with entire decades going by without the publication of a single piece of news about Tristan da Cunha. When, at the turn of the century, the situation seems to be finally improving, the outbreak of two world conflicts ends up overshadowing the island and pushing it, once again, into oblivion.

The second is an issue of quality, therefore of representation. Being part of a monologue, more than a dialogue, the news pieces end up providing their own image of Tristan, which, at least in the 19th century, is an idealised and oversimplified picture that is not representative of the difficulties of colonising an isolated island. A turning point, however, occurs around the 1910s, when the peculiarities of some island traditions, together with the Crown's assumption of responsibility, start triggering the press' interest, resulting in the publication of more detailed news pieces that, eventually, break the idealised frame and do justice to the remarkable achievements of this community of people.

Overall, this study has attempted to show how the dialogue of cultures, even when unequal in nature and when involving unequal communities, has the potential of raising awareness on specific issues and, eventually, of improving the living conditions of a community.

References

Brander, Jan: *Tristan da Cunha 1506–1902*. Allen & Unwin: London 1940.

Crawford, Allan: *I Went to Tristan*. Allen & Unwin: London 1941.

Crawford, Allan: *Tristan da Cunha and the Roaring Forties*. Allen & Unwin: London 1982.

Evans, Dorothy: *Schooling in the South Atlantic Islands 1661–1992*. Anthony Nelson: Oswestry 1994.

Facchinetti, Roberta (ed.): *Corpus Linguistics: Twenty-Five Years on*. Rodopi: Amsterdam 2007.

Facchinetti, Roberta/Brownlees, Nicholas/Bös, Birte/Fries, Udo: *News as Changing Texts: Corpora, Methodologies and Analysis. Second Edition*. Cambridge Scholars Publishing: Cambridge, Newcastle-upon-Tyne 2015.

Marchi, Anna/Taylor Charlotte: "Establishing the EU: The Representation of Europe in the Press in 1993 and 2005". In: Jucker, Andreas H./Schreier,

Daniel/Hundt, Marianne (eds.) *Corpora: Pragmatics and Discourse: Papers from the 29th International Conference on English Language Research on Computerized Corpora (ICAME 29)*. Rodopi: Amsterdam 2009, pp. 203–226.

Munch, Peter A.: *Sociology of Tristan da Cunha (Results of the Norwegian Scientific Expedition to Tristan da Cunha, 1937–1938)*. Norske Videnskaps-Akademi: Oslo 1945.

Munch, Peter A.: *Crisis in Utopia: The Ordeal of Tristan da Cunha*. Crowell: New York 1971.

Schreier, Daniel: *Isolation and Language Change: Contemporary and Sociohistorical Evidence from Tristan da Cunha English*. Palgrave Macmillan: New York 2003.

Schreier, Daniel: "Tristan da Cunha English". In: Schreier, Daniel/Trudgill, Peter/Schneider, Edgar W./Williams, Jeffrey P. (eds.): *The Lesser-Known Varieties of English*. Cambridge University Press: Cambridge 2010.

Schreier, Daniel/Lavarello-Schreier, Karen: *Tristan da Cunha and the Tristanians*. Battlebridge Publications: London 2011.

Schreier, Daniel/Trudgill, Peter: "The segmental phonology of nineteenth century Tristan da Cunha English: Convergence and local innovation". *English Language and Linguistics*, 10, 2006, pp. 119–141.

Trudgill, Peter: *Dialects in Contact*. Blackwell: Oxford 1986.

Trudgill, Peter: *New-Dialect Formation: The Inevitability of Colonial Englishes*. Oxford University Press: Oxford 2004.

Wace, Nigel M./Holdgate Martin W.: *Man and Nature in the Tristan da Cunha Islands*. International Union for Conservation of Nature and Natural Resources: Morges 1976.

Zettersten, Anne: *The English of Tristan da Cunha*. Gleerup: Lund 1969.

Biographien

Enrico Battaglia nasce a Bassano del Grappa nel 1990. Dopo la maturità artistica si iscrive al corso di laurea in Discipline delle Arti della Musica e dello Spettacolo dell'Università di Padova. Si laurea nel 2013 con la tesi "Bill Viola un ponte tra passato e presente" che esplora la relazione tra le arti multimediali e le arti rinascimentali.

Nel 2012 durante l'esperienza Erasmus a Murcia (Spagna) si appassiona alla divulgazione di tematiche sociali attraverso la comunicazione visiva, che ha modo di approfondire poi presso il corso di laurea di Design e arti della Libera Università di Bolzano a cui si iscrive nel 2014. "Fuori di qui" è il progetto di *graphic journalism* con cui si laurea nel 2016, la cui idea nasce con la partecipazione al *workshop* internazionale Esodoc (*European Social Documentary*).

In seguito approfondisce in Germania lo storytelling e la comunicazione visiva lavorando come Graphic animator nella produzione di un documentario che tratta il tema dello sfruttamento degli operai indiani a Dubai. Attualmente vive a Padova dove si occupa di *motion design* e *web*.

Email: enricobattaglia.net@gmail.com

Marcella Cometti (06.06.1991) – a luglio 2016 dottoressa in Giurisprudenza – percorso europeo e transnazionale- con votazione 110/110 presso l'Università degli Studi di Trento. Ad oggi, tirocinante presso l'UNHCR (Alto Commissariato delle Nazioni Unite per i Rifugiati), Protection Unit.

Da ottobre 2016 a giugno 2017 operatrice d'accoglienza ed operatrice legale presso la Cooperativa Olinda (orientamento, formazione ed assistenza del richiedente asilo durante lo svolgimento della procedura per il riconoscimento della protezione internazionale ed espletamento delle pratiche amministrative legali).

Il suo percorso formativo è caratterizzato dall'approfondimento ed interesse per la legislazione in materia di immigrazione: da ottobre 2013 a febbraio 2014 frequenta la Hebrew University a Gerusalemme, dove ha la possibilità di approfondire le problematiche della politica immigratoria israeliana.

A settembre 2014 frequenta il Corso di Alta formazione sul diritto degli stranieri tenuto dall'Associazione per gli Studi Giuridici sull'Immigrazione (ASGI) presso la Scuola Superiore Sant'Anna di Pisa; tale Corso ha il fine di offrire un quadro generale della legislazione e della giurisprudenza in tema di immigrazione e asilo.

La sua carriera universitaria si conclude nel luglio 2016 con una tesi di ricerca riguardante il diritto al ricongiungimento familiare dei beneficiari di protezione internazionale (ricerca in parte realizzata a Copenaghen grazie all'attribuzione di una borsa di studio del Centro Europeo di Eccellenza Jean Monnet).

Da ottobre 2015 a maggio 2016 frequenta, a Roma, la Scuola di Alta Formazione per operatori legali specializzati in protezione internazionale (ASGI).

Email: comettimarcella@gmail.com

Valerio Fidenzi is a PhD student in English Linguistics and Historical Journalism at the University of Verona, where he is also teaching assistant of English Language and History of the English Language. After spending one year at the University of Cambridge as part of his MA programme, he graduated in Publishing and Journalism in 2016 and was awarded *summa cum laude* for his thesis "Tristan da Cunha: Sociolinguistics and News reporting on the World's Remotest Island". This work inspired him to set up a research project centred on the representation of the other in historical journalism. Besides the island of Tristan da Cunha, he is currently working on the representation of colonies such as Canada, China and India in one of the world's most influential publications: the weekly magazine-format newspaper *The Economist*.

Valerio Fidenzi è un dottorando di ricerca in Linguistica inglese e Storia del giornalismo all'Università degli Studi di Verona, dove ricopre anche il ruolo di cultore della materia in Lingua inglese e Storia della lingua inglese. Dopo aver trascorso un anno presso l'Università di Cambridge come parte del suo percorso di studi in Editoria e Giornalismo, nel 2016 ha conseguito la laurea magistrale con una tesi, premiata con la menzione della lode, dal titolo "Tristan da Cunha: Sociolinguistics and Newsreporting on the World's Remotest Island". Questo lavoro l'ha portato a sviluppare un progetto di ricerca incentrato sulla rappresentazione dell'altro nei giornali storici di lingua anglofona. Oltre all'isola di Tristan da Cunha, si sta attualmente occupando della rappresentazione di colonie come il Canada, la Cina e l'India in una delle testate più influenti al mondo: il settimanale inglese *The Economist*.

Email: valerio.fidenzi@univr.it

Dennis Fricken, MSc., geboren 1985 in Norden, studierte Geographie an den Universitäten Osnabrück und Innsbruck mit den Schwerpunkten Stadt- und Regionalentwicklung sowie Entwicklungsforschung. Im Rahmen seiner Masterarbeit am Institut für Geographie in Innsbruck befasste er sich mit dem Thema „Amenity Migration" im Hohen Atlas in Marokko. Für die Forschung erhielt er ein Stipendium der Universität Innsbruck für kurzfristige wissenschaftliche Arbeiten im Ausland. Dabei untersuchte er die siedlungsgeographischen, ökonomischen, ökologischen und sozialen Auswirkungen dieser als Wohlstandsmigration zu charakterisierenden Migrationsbewegungen in einem marokkanischen Berberdorf. Die Masterarbeit wurde beim 5. JungakademikerInnen-Forum „Kulturen im Dialog" in Südtirol an der Freien Universität Bozen vorgestellt und fand Eingang im Sammelband „Global Amenity Migration: Transforming Rural Culture, Economy and Landscape" (2014, Hrsg.: Moss/Glorioso). Im Anschluss an sein erfolgreich abgeschlossenes Studium arbeitete er in Innsbruck in den Bereichen Klimaschutz, Klimawandelanpassung und Mobilität. Seit 2017 ist er im Landkreis Ludwigsburg als Klimaschutzmanager tätig.

Dennis Fricken, MSc., born 1985 in Norden, studied Geography at the Universities of Osnabrück and Innsbruck. His research focuses are urban and regional development and development research. His master thesis at the Department of Geography addressed the phenomenon of amenity migration in the High Atlas in Morocco. For this research he got a short-term grant abroad. He analysed the socio-economic, ecological and cultural impacts of amenity migration in a Moroccan Berber village. The master thesis was presented at the Fifth Forum of Young Graduates in South Tyrol and was published in "Global Amenity Migration: Transforming Rural Culture, Economy and Landscape" (2014, eds.: Moss/Glorioso). After he successfully completed his studies, he worked in Innsbruck in the fields of climate protection, climate change adaption and mobility. Since 2017, he works as a climate protection manager in the county of Ludwigsburg.

Email: dennis.fricken@ewetel.net

Daniela Gruber, Mag.a, geboren 1984 in Meran, ist PhD-Studentin an der Universität Innsbruck am Institut für Soziologie und arbeitet zum Thema Migration in Südtirol. Ihre Forschungsschwerpunkte sind Migration, Minderheiten, Transnationalismus und Religionsethnologie. Ihr Diplomstudium am Institut für Kultur- und Sozialanthropologie an der Universität Wien beendete sie mit ihrer Arbeit über transnationale religiöse Netzwerke von Roma und Sinti. Basis der Arbeit waren Forschungsaufenthalte in Frankreich und Österreich. Für die Forschung in Frankreich erhielt sie ein Stipendium für kurzfristiges

wissenschaftliches Arbeiten im Ausland von der Universität Wien. Die Diplomarbeit wurde beim 5. JungakademikerInnen-Forum in Südtirol „Kulturen im
Dialog" an der Freien Universität Bozen vorgestellt, sowie bei der Jahrestagung
der SEG (Schweizer Ethnologische Gesellschaft) in Lausanne. Daniela Gruber
arbeitete als Forschungsbeauftragte der Freien Universität Bozen und ist zur-
zeit für das Sprachenzentrum in Meran tätig. Während ihres Studiums war sie
redaktionelle Mitarbeiterin bei der Menschenrechtsorganisation „Bedrohte Völker" in Wien.

Daniela Gruber, Mag.a, born in 1984 in Meran, is a PhD student at the Innsbruck University, Department of Sociology. Her research topics are migration,
minorities, transnationalism and ethnology of religion. She completed her
diploma studies at the Department of Social and Cultural Anthropology, University of Vienna, with her diploma thesis on transnational religious networks
of Roma and Sinti. The thesis is based on research stays in Austria and France.
For the research in France she got a short-term grant abroad. The diploma
thesis was presented at the Fifth Forum for Young Graduates in South Tyrol,
and at the annual conference of the Swiss Anthropological Association in Lausanne. Daniela Gruber worked as a commissioned researcher at the Free University of Bolzano and is currently working at the Language Centre in Meran.
During her studies in Vienna, she worked for editorial efforts at the human
rights organization "Bedrohte Völker" in Vienna.

Email: daniela.gruber@gmx.com

Mihaela Mihova, 1990 in Varna geboren, hat schon früh ihre Leidenschaft für
Sprachen entdeckt. Sie hat in Sofia begonnen Skandinavistik zu studieren, ein
Auslandssemester in Umeå absolviert und das Bachelorstudium in Wien abge-
schlossen. Danach widmete sie sich dem Masterstudium Deutsch als Zweit- und
Fremdsprache an der Universität Wien und untersuchte im Rahmen dessen die
Stellung der deutschen Sprache in Schweden. Die Inspiration für diesen Bereich
entstammte zum einen aus der Aktualität des Themas und zum anderen aus dem
Wunsch, die Schwerpunkte des Bachelor- und Masterstudiums zu kombinieren.

Mihova unterrichtet seit 2014 Schwedisch und Deutsch am Sprachenzentrum
der Universität Wien, war außerdem während ihres Studiums Tutorin für skan-
dinavistische Literaturwissenschaft und für DaF/DaZ an den Instituten für Ver-
gleichende Literaturwissenschaft und Germanistik.

Mihaela Mihova was born in 1990 in Varna, Bulgaria. Already as a child she
discovered her passion for languages. Mihova studied Scandinavian Studies

at the University of Sofia, but after one year she moved to Vienna where she graduated at the University of Vienna. She also did an Erasmus exchange in Umeå, Sweden. Following this, Mihova dedicated herself to the master's program German as a Foreign and Second language at the University of Vienna. Within these studies, she researched the role of the German language in Sweden for her master's thesis. The inspiration for this issue came from its actuality as well as the personal desire to combine the main areas of her bachelor's and master's studies.

Since 2014 Mihova has been teaching Swedish and German at the Language Centre of the University of Vienna. Furthermore, during her studies she worked as tutor for Scandinavian literature and later for German as a Foreign and Second Language at the Institutes for Comparative Literature and German Studies.

Email: mail@mihaelamihova.com

Federica Pastore graduated from Alma Mater Studiorum with a bachelor's degree in Foreign Languages and Literature and a dissertation in Political and Economic Geography. During her Erasmus stay at Trinity College Dublin in 2015–2016 she very much appreciated the course on "Multilingualism" and got interested in themes such as language policies, immigration and identity. She is enrolled in a master's degree in International Cooperation for the Conservation of Ethno-Cultural Heritage in Ravenna, where she also volunteered teaching Italian to immigrants. Currently she is doing an Internship in Berlin at Migration Hub, where she is learning a lot about integration and social entrepreneurship.

Email: federica.pastore@studio.unibo.it

Stefano Piccioni, nasce nel 1979 a Milano città nella quale si laurea in Psicologia dell'età evolutiva prima e in Scienze pedagogiche poi all'università di Milano-Bicocca. Utilizza gli strumenti acquisiti nella sua formazione come educatore, pedagogista, supervisore, coordinatore, formatore, docente, progettista. Ha collaborato con enti pubblici e strutture private del Terzo settore. Attualmente svolge il ruolo di pedagogista/educatore all'interno della Neuropsichiatria infantile della Fondazione IRCCS Ca' Granda – Ospedale Maggiore Policlinico di Milano. Coordina e supervisiona progetti inerenti l'ambito della disabilità per la Società Cooperativa Sociale Sociosfera Onlus e per l'Associazione di volontariato La Fabbrica di Milano.

Email: s.piccioni@campus.unimib.it

Roberta Rosa graduated in European and International Studies from the School of International Studies – University of Trento. She presented a final thesis in European and international law and comparative constitutional law of minority protection, combining a both theoretical and empirical method, thus analysing literature and legal sources.

She is a former trainee at the Institute for Comparative Federalism of Eurac Research (Bolzano) where she took part in the research titled "Bridge building and integration in diverse societies", conducted in cooperation with the European Centre for Minority Issues of Flensburg (Germany) for the OSCE High Commissioner on National Minorities.

Email: roberta.rosa29@gmail.com

Interkultureller Dialog

Herausgegeben von Annemarie Profanter

Band 1   Annemarie Profanter (Hrsg./dir./ed.): Kulturen im Dialog - Culture in Dialogo - Cultures in Dialogue. Erstes JungakademikerInnen-Forum in Südtirol. Primo Forum per Neolaureati in Alto Adige. First Forum for Young Graduates in South Tyrol. 2010.

Band 2   Martina Rienzner: Interkulturelle Kommunikation im Asylverfahren. 2011.

Band 3   Annemarie Profanter (Hrsg./dir./ed.): Kulturen im Dialog II - Culture in Dialogo II - Cultures in Dialogue II. Zweites JungakademikerInnen-Forum in Südtirol. Secondo Forum per Neolaureati in Alto Adige. Second Forum for Young Graduates in South Tyrol. 2011.

Band 4   Peter Volgger: between & betwixt. Transurbane Lebenswelten in Bozen. 2013.

Band 5   Annemarie Profanter (Hrsg./dir./ed.): Kulturen im Dialog III - Culture in Dialogo III - Cultures in Dialogue III. Drittes JungakademikerInnen-Forum in Südtirol. Terzo Forum per Neolaureati in Alto Adige. Third Forum for Young Graduates in South Tyrol. 2014.

Band 6   Giulia Cordin: Narrative Design. The Designer as an Instigator of Changes. With an Introduction by Formafantasma. 2016.

Band 7   Annemarie Profanter (Hrsg./dir./ed.): Kulturen im Dialog IV - Culture in Dialogo IV - Cultures in Dialogue IV. Viertes JungakademikerInnen-Forum in Südtirol. Quarto Forum per Neolaureati in Alto Adige. Fourth Forum for Young Graduates in South Tyrol. 2016.

Band 8   Annemarie Profanter (Hrsg./dir./ed.): Kulturen im Dialog V - Culture in Dialogo V - Cultures in Dialogue V. Fünftes JungakademikerInnen-Forum in Südtirol. Quinto Forum per Neolaureati in Alto Adige. Fifth Forum for Young Graduates in South Tyrol. 2019.

www.peterlang.com

www.ingramcontent.com/pod-product-compliance
Lightning Source LLC
Chambersburg PA
CBHW041931260326
41914CB00010B/1259